The Philosophy of Composition

E.D. Hirsch, Jr.

The University of Chicago Press / Chicago and London

The Philosophy of Composition

The University of Chicago Press, Chicago 60637
The University of Chicago Press, Ltd., London

Library of Congress Cataloging in Publication Data

Hirsch, Eric Donald.
    The philosophy of composition.

    Includes index.
    1.   English language—Rhetoric—Study and
teaching. I.   Title.
PE1403.H57   808'.001   77-4944
ISBN 0-226-34242-5

E. D. HIRSCH, JR., Kenan Professor of English at
the University of Virginia, stepped down from the
department chairmanship in 1970 to become director of composition. Among his extensive publications in literary history, linguistic and
hermeneutic theory, and semantics are *The Aims
of Interpretation*, *Validity in Interpretation*,
Innocence and Experience, and *Wordsworth and
Schelling*.

To my fellow composition teachers

The maxims contained in works on composition and rhetoric are presented in an unorganized form. Standing as isolated dogmas—as empirical generalizations, they are neither so clearly apprehended, nor so much respected, as they would be were they deduced from some simple first principle.

Herbert Spencer,
"The Philosophy of Style," 1852

Contents

Preface

Preface

Some readers of this book will be familiar with Poe's essay called "The Philosophy of Composition," which surveys the principles of beauty in lyric poetry. They will rightly suspect that my allusion to Poe's title carries a touch of irony, since my subject is the more prosaic one of composition teaching in schools and colleges. But the mild irony is directed not just to my own, humbler subject, but also to Poe's aestheticism. For I write as one converted from aestheticism to the more practical side of an English teacher's responsibilities. Perhaps a brief account of how I came to write the book will help explain its character.

My conversion experience occurred about eight years ago, near the end of my term as chairman of a university English department, when I was preparing the annual budget. I began to wonder how long our university would continue its big expenditures on literary teaching and scholarship without insisting that we devote comparable energies to the teaching that was paying for so many of our literary courses—namely the teaching of composition. At the same time, I felt ashamed of my neglect of composition during my chairmanship, and I asked my successor to name me to my present job—director of composition.

I then began, over seven years ago, an intensive study of research in the field. I found the subject more complex and challenging than any which I had undertaken in literary history or literary theory. Still, I hoped that my previous work in theory of interpretation might be useful in pursuing composition research, since interpretation—or reading—is obviously correlative to writing. But after many years of work on composition, I can see that my hopes were misplaced, and that this book bears very little relation to my previous literary research. Its shortcomings and virtues are those to be expected, no doubt, from an author who enters a new field in middle age.

I should say one thing more about my title. Although *the* philosophy of composition sounds comprehensive, I have omitted some important subjects—for instance the subject of invention. Nonetheless, I have kept Poe's ambitious title, because the book argues for certain privileged goals in the teaching of literacy. It claims that an authentic ideology of literacy inheres in the subject itself, and should guide our teaching of it. This privileged ideology is the common ground on which we can all stand in our common enterprise. That is the sense in which I have thought it appropriate to speak of *the* philosophy of composition.

In writing the book, I have received generous help from institutions and colleagues. In 1971 I received a yearlong fellowship from the National Endowment for the Humanities which enabled me to continue my linguistic studies. In 1975 I received a grant from the University of Virginia to cover the expenses of preparing the manuscript. I am grateful to both institutions for their assistance. Several colleagues have made helpful comments on the first version of the manuscript, and I wish to thank in particular Lester Beaurline, Donald Gray, Polly Hirsch, Robert Kellogg, John McGalliard, Ellen Nold, Charlene Sedgwick, Ross Winterowd, and Richard Young. I also wish to express my thanks for the help given me by many composition teachers at diverse schools and colleges. To these teachers and to their fellow workers in the vineyard I have dedicated this book.

Introduction

Introduction

The Scope and Purpose of This Book

This book is addressed mainly to teachers of composition and other professional students of prose, including authors of composition handbooks. It is not a handbook itself, nor a classroom guide for teachers. Many of its implications for teaching are indirect, especially in those areas where too little is known to permit authoritative conclusions about teaching methods. In the last chapters, the book does hazard some concrete suggestions about writing and teaching, but the rest of it deals with a more general subject that might be called "the linguistics of literacy."[1]

Within this large subject, the chief matters addressed by the book are those that connect linguistics, psycholinguistics, and historical philology with the goals of composition teaching. I ask and attempt to answer the following questions: What are the distinctive features of written, as compared with oral, speech? What universal tendencies are observable in the historical development of prose? Can we determine by such linguistic and

---

1. Normally, the word *literacy* means proficiency in reading and in forming letters. In this book, I use the word to embrace also the ability to write extended, communicative discourse. For precision, I also use the phrases "oral speech" and "written speech," instead of "speech and writing" or "spoken and written language." I have wanted to preserve Saussure's important distinction between *parole* (or "speech") and *langue* (or "language.") *Parole* means a *use* of language, while *langue* means an abstract system of linguistic possibilities. An example of written language would be a word in a dictionary, but its definition would be written speech.

historical analyses the universal characteristics of good prose, and thence the most appropriate goals for teaching composition? If so, what specific knowledge must we have in order to attain those teaching goals? More particularly, what are the psycholinguistic bases of good prose, and how can our knowledge of these psycholinguistic principles lead to progress in teaching composition? Finally, can these and other theoretical principles lead to the valid assessment of writing ability, and so enable us to evaluate the effectiveness of different teaching methods?

These questions and the answers to them which I propose in the following pages obviously cover only a part of the linguistics of literacy. But I believe that they are the most important questions to be asked about composition at the present time. Over eight years ago, when I began to devote almost all my research time to this subject, our present crisis in literacy was already hatching. Our most urgent problem seemed then, and continues to seem now, the lack of direction in our teaching and research. We are beset by conflicting ideologies which confuse us and hamper progress in both domains. So I think we must answer hard questions about the goals of composition teaching and research before we can work out the best ways of achieving those goals. In the course of my studies, I have come to think that answers to some of our questions about goals can be determined from the nature and history of writing, rather than from ideology and personal taste—two potent sources of our conflicts over goals.

Another source of conflict has been empirical uncertainty. We simply have known too little about the psychology and pedagogy of composition to get definitive answers to most of our practical questions. Ideology always holds greatest sway where knowledge is least. Emotion and dogma rush in to fill the gap left by uncertainty. The questions about composition that I have chosen to ask and have tried to answer in this book are those which seem to be the most pressing questions within this context of ideological conflict and empirical uncertainty. The whole of Chapter 2, for instance, implicitly addresses itself to the dispute over teaching a "standard dialect" at the expense of "nonstandard dialects." In that chapter I show that much of our debate is empirically misconceived, and that our ideological disagreements tend to diminish when the linguistic and historical facts are accurately described.

Moreover, literacy tends to foster its own authentic ideology.

The goal of linguistic normalization, for instance, is inherent in mass education and is implicit in the very concept of giving instruction in writing. Self-conscious efforts toward normalization have at all times characterized every educational program in every literate culture of the world.[2] This historical tendency could be resisted, of course, but the result would be logical and practical incoherence, and social harm as well.

At some point, it is true, value choices have to be made. Not everything is decidable by neutral linguistic facts and dominant historical tendencies. But suppose the historical tendencies of literacy *are* inevitable? I admit that no one can certainly know this, but if the historical tendencies are not only inevitable but also desirable, then only harm can come from resisting them. The structure of this historical argument is of course Marxist, but the fallibility of Marxism is not in the structure of its argument. If political Marxism is wrong, the fault lies in its premises, some of which are historical premises and not just ideological ones. The validity of all such historical theses about goals depends at least in part upon the validity of the facts adduced in their favor.

The present book does defend a particular goal in the teaching of composition, but it also gives careful empirical support to the stand that it takes. I believe that the empirical evidence which I have adduced and interpreted has raised my argument above mere ideology. This scholarly emphasis in the book will, I hope, persuade the majority of composition teachers that its point of view is linguistically and historically correct.

I also hope that even those who remain unpersuaded by my point of view will find the scholarship informative and useful. Some of the materials which I have applied to composition have been ignored in past discussions of the subject, while other materials, particularly in psycholinguistics, are too new to have been assimilated. I hope that all composition teachers will find these materials of interest and use.

Recent Neglect of the Linguistics of Literacy

The empirical uncertainty that we composition teachers complain of is not the fault of our much-maligned schools of

---

2. See. M. M. Guxman, "Some General Regularities in the Formation and Development of National Languages," in *Readings in the Sociology of Language*, ed. J. A. Fishman (The Hague, 1968), pp. 766–84.

education. Every year these institutions sponsor numerous theses and articles on the pedagogy of composition. Yet our uncertainty persists because this applied research gets little direct support from basic work in foundational subjects like linguistics.

Ever since 1933, the study of written speech has been a low-status subject in linguistics. That was the year when Bloomfield, the most influential writer on linguistics before Chomsky, attempted to give the subject a new orientation by departing rigorously from the old philological emphasis on the written word. In 1933, Bloomfield considered the general science of linguistics to be "only in its beginnings," because it had only begun to realize that written speech had no independent linguistic authority. His disdain of writing was summarized in the famous remark "Writing is not language, but merely a way of recording language by means of visible marks."[3] This opinion, while not unchallenged, is still dominant. As John Lyons correctly observed in his *Introduction to Theoretical Linguistics*, "It is one of the fundamental assumptions of modern linguistics that sound, not writing, is the primary medium of language."[4] Under this dominant view, important work on the subject of written speech has been rare since Bloomfield's day.

Similarly, in departments of language and literature, the purely philological study of written language has fallen into relative neglect. Just as Bloomfield stressed the primary importance of oral speech, literary theorists since the 1930s have stressed the primary importance of artistic form. Linguistic analysis in literary scholarship has been mainly aimed at stylistic analysis. Again, there are honorable exceptions, but on the whole, the philological study of written speech has become vestigial in departments of literature.

Modern society at large, however, has continued to take just the opposite point of view. Society places the highest priority on written speech and the teaching of reading and writing. Theorists of grammar are generously supported by society in the hope that the subject can be directly useful in the teaching of composition. Departments of English in American universities are large and expensive not because they foster instruction and research in literary art but because they teach composition. This discordance between the utilitarian values of society and the intellectual

3. L. Bloomfield, *Language* (New York, 1933), p. 31.
4. J. Lyons, *Introduction to Theoretical Linguistics* (Cambridge, England, 1968), p. 7.

pursuits of scholars is not necessarily scandalous or surprising, but I do think that a contributing cause of the recent decline in literacy has been a decline of interest in the subject on the part of the most talented and prestigious scholars in linguistics and literary study.

Let me provide a homely example of the disconnection between the preoccupations of higher research and the needs of instruction in literacy. The teacher of composition at a university normally uses some kind of textbook as a guide for himself and his students. The writer of the textbook is normally a professor of literature whose competence to compose such a guide to instruction has been gained by trial and error in the classroom. He has no comprehensive knowledge of those subjects which can provide an answer to the following question: "What is the most effective way to teach the skill of writing?" New theories about the answer to this question find their way into the textbooks every year, and their very proliferation proclaims their insufficiency and the paucity of the basic research behind them. The discontinuity between high-status goals in research and high-priority goals in instruction can be seen very strikingly in the amateurish world of composition textbooks.

The neglect of basic research in composition has encouraged us to be our own oracles in the classroom. If really authoritative guidance were available, most of us would follow it, and be less inclined to grasp desperately at each new "approach" that comes along. I believe that our lack of authoritative knowledge has created more conflicts among us than all our differences of taste and ideology. This book does not pretend to provide that authoritative and encompassing knowledge, but, in offering the fruits of several years of research, it does aim to encourage a conviction that we *can* gain that authoritative knowledge within a decade.

Summary of This Book

Since the argument of the book is cumulative, it is best read according to the instructions given to the White Rabbit by the King of Hearts: "Begin at the beginning, and go on till you come to the end: then stop." But since some readers may wish to consult isolated chapters, and since others may wish to have from the start a clear sense of the whole, I shall summarize the main arguments here. What is thereby lost from the drama of gradual revelation may be added to security of communication.

The first chapter is partly designed to counter Bloomfield's influential doctrine that writing is merely a secondary representation of speech. Progress in the linguistics of literacy and in composition research requires that this oversimplification be corrected. The chapter summarizes previous work on the relations between oral and written speech, and concludes that all of the most important points were made early in this century by Henry Bradley. One of Bradley's observations is a direct reversal of Bloomfield's doctrine: In literate societies, Bradley observed, writing is sometimes the *primary* substance of speech and, in those cases, oral speech is a secondary representation of writing!

In relation to composition, the chief distinction between oral and written speech is a functional distinction. Some composition handbooks admonish students to write naturally, as they speak— Bloomfieldian advice which overlooks the functional distinctions between speech and writing. For oral speech normally takes place in a concrete situation that supplies external, extra-verbal clues to meaning, while written speech, lacking this dimension, is able to communicate effectively only if it supplies much of its context within the verbal medium alone. Hence, for native speakers, the chief difficulty in learning to write well is in learning how to use language in an unaccustomed way. The functional peculiarity of writing is its need to furnish its own context.

Chapter 2 addresses, among other topics, the debate over standard versus nonstandard language. This topic is placed in the context of linguistic change. The chapter points out that while "nonstandard" dialects continue to change significantly in grammar and phonology, the standard language does not so change. (Lexical change is not the crucial issue here.) Some linguists have too flatly asserted that all languages change, and while this was indeed true of written English through the mid-eighteenth century, it has not been true of English grammar and phonology since that time. Because of the conservatism of literacy, Standard English is unlikely ever again to change significantly in grammar or phonology, as long as universal schooling persists.

Besides this conservatism and stability, all the standard literate languages have other special characteristics which distinguish them from any oral dialect. Hence, it is a sociolinguistic mistake to view a standard language as merely class dialect. Some sociolinguists have therefore coined the term *grapholect* to indicate that standard written languages are different in *kind* from oral dialects. This terminological distinction shows that the standard languages are properly *hors de combat* with oral dialects, and the distinction also removes the whole issue of bi-dialectism from the teaching of literacy. The inherent and necessary direction of mass literacy is towards the dominance of the standard languages of the world.

By the end of these two chapters, the exposition has implicitly established two goals of composition teaching. First, by establishing a functional distinction between oral and written speech, Chapter 1 has implied that students should be taught how to make their writing self-contextual. Second, by establishing the normative character of writing, Chapter 2 has implied that students should be taught the grammatical conventions of the standard language as being the correct standards for writing. But so far, the discussion has not implied stylistic goals for composition teaching. Since good prose is written in a variety of styles, what stylistic principles should take precedence? This question has been the subject of vigorous debates in both Britain and America, with one side stressing the importance of lively, self-expressive writing and the other stressing the superior virtues of cogency and clarity. Many teachers make a compromise between the two stylistic goals on the grounds that certain stylistic virtues are more important in some kinds of writing than in others. Can these various positions be reconciled or resolved? That is the question to which the next chapter is implicitly addressed.

Again, the question is set in a general historical perspective. The third chapter attempts to show that despite the stylistic variety found in the history of prose, the tendency of that history has been towards increasing efficiency of communication in all genres of writing. A text is said to be more efficient than another if it requires less effort by the reader in understanding the very same meaning.

The chapter argues that the tendency towards increased communicative efficiency is a universal tendency in the history of all languages. This "progressive" theory of language change has been illustrated by Jespersen, documented by Zipf, and strongly reinforced in recent years by Martinet. I argue that this progressive tendency in the general history of languages can be seen also in the general history of English prose. In all genres of writing, including those with intricate and difficult styles, the trend has been to achieve the same effects with less and less reader effort. It is possible to make this comparative judgment by virtue of recent discoveries in the psychology of language processing. This psychological research has yielded universals which apply to all

languages at all historical periods. With reference to these
psychological universals, the progressive tendency of prose style is
unmistakable.

From these considerations, I infer that there are universal
stylistic features in all good prose of every kind and that these
features of good style are all reducible to a single principle: One
prose style is better than another when it communicates the same
meanings as the other does but requires less effort from the
reader. Since this stylistic principle is tolerant of every conceiv-
able semantic intention in prose, it does not favor any single prose
style. Intentional elegance, intentional obscurity, and intentional
lucidity are equally governed by the principle. Moreover, the
principle itself is grounded in linguistic history and in universals
of human psychology.

The name that I give this stylistic principle is "relative readability." "Readability" refers to the easiness with which a reader
understands a text, while "relative" explicitly concedes the fact
that easiness must vary with different semantic intentions. This is
the subject taken up in Chapter 4. The first extensive discussion of
this stylistic principle was written by Herbert Spencer and
published in 1852. His essay has never been superseded, and
recent psychological research has confirmed many of his brilliant
conjectures.

After giving a brief account of Spencer's theories, the chapter
describes current research on readability and criticizes the limitations of readability formulas. The chapter aims to describe with
some precision what is meant by "relative readability" and also to
suggest that this principle coincides with our intuitive criteria for
judging the stylistic excellence of prose. In sum, this chapter,
together with the preceding one, attempts to establish relative
readability as our common stylistic goal in teaching composition.

Accepting the goal is one thing; attaining it is another, more
difficult thing. The next chapter, which focuses on the actual
components of readability, is undoubtedly the most difficult
chapter in the book, as well as the longest. It summarizes what
has been learned about the psychological bases of readability.
The subsequent application of these results to actual teaching will
require a lot of experimenting, and the basic research itself will
need to be carried further. Hence the chapter is in many places
an interim report, and in other places it is speculative. Nonetheless, some results do seem to be firmly established, and these have
great significance for the teaching of composition.

Probably the most important results are those which pertain to the operations of memory in language processing. When we are reading a clause, we must briefly store up a certain number of words and phrases whose semantic-syntactic properties have not yet been fully determined. Only later do these properties become determined—when we have come to understand the clause as a whole. But our ability to store up not-yet-determined words and phrases is very limited. The capacity of our short-term memory is about five unitary items, whether these be words or phrases. An understanding of this narrow psychological limit will probably help both teachers and students to understand the character of readability in a clause.

A second important relationship between memory and readability involves long-term memory. In general, the earlier parts of a text are stored by the reader in a nonlinguistic form. This means that under ordinary circumstances a reader cannot be depended on to remember the actual phrasing of earlier parts of a text. Style as such is short-lived. Linguistic form begins to decay in memory after about twelve seconds. Yet memory for the *meaning* of earlier parts of a text is very tenacious and relatively accurate. This means, as a practical matter, that readability in prose will depend on the author's making direct verbal connections over rather short stretches. Only a few important and repeated words or phrases will be directly remembered over long stretches of discourse.

These two samples will suffice to indicate the kind of materials dealt with in Chapter 5. To anyone concerned with the very pulse of the machine—the psychological checks and balances of readable prose—this chapter may be the most interesting part of the book. But interest may be mingled with dissatisfaction, for, although some principles are known, many remain unknown or uncertain and their practical applications unexplored. Nonetheless, from what *is* known, some practical inferences can be drawn, and these are the subject of the next chapter.

In this penultimate chapter, I give some practical advice about composition teaching to the extent that this advice seems warranted by our present knowledge. If I avoid speculation about many details of great importance, that is because I want the book to be a reliable guide to the topics that it treats. One of the great drawbacks of practical composition handbooks is their unreliable and speculative character owing to the limited research on which their advice is based. In the present state of our knowledge, the more detailed the advice the more likely it is to be wrong.

Nonetheless, I do venture to draw practical conclusions on the following points: the most effective way to put composition into the curriculum; the most important maxims of prose and their relation to psychological principles; the most effective techniques of classroom teaching; the most important principles to keep in mind when choosing and writing composition textbooks; and, finally, the most promising lines of composition research.

To devote my last words to research seemed to be the best way to end the book. Well-conceived, reliable research is the thing most needful for teachers of composition. We already know enough to foresee the practical utility of a serious research effort. And of all the research problems which we face, the one most deserving of our attention is the problem of writing assessment. Until we have reliable means of rating the quality of a student's prose, we lack a sound basis for determining the teaching methods which will raise that quality most efficiently. In other words, we cannot progress in other lines of pedagogical research until we solve the assessment problem. The final practical suggestions of the book concern assessment research. In the last chapter, I suggest an approach that could lead to a sensitive, sophisticated method of rating prose, yet one that is not just sophisticated but also valid, universal, quick, and highly reliable. To achieve this, however, the criteria *behind* the rating system would need to be agreed upon. In earlier chapters of this book, I advocate the criterion of relative readability. If that standard should be widely accepted, the assessment problem could probably be solved, to the great benefit of composition research and composition teaching.

1 Distinctive Features of Written Speech

Distinctive Features of Written Speech

Leading Ideas in the Study of Written Speech

The important research on written speech divides into two general categories: the historical study of physical scripts and the functional study of writing as a special kind of speech. Obviously the second, semantically oriented sort of study has the greater interest for the linguistics of literacy, but the two strands of research cannot be completely disentangled. The nature of a script, whether ideographic, syllabic, or alphabetic, will have an immense influence on the subsequent history of the spoken language and also on the spread of literacy.

The obvious case in point is Chinese, which uses an ideographic script that presently encompasses at least 44,000 characters. While some of these characters contain phonetic elements which represent certain sounds of Chinese during one of its stages, the system as a whole is relatively independent of spoken Chinese. As a consequence, the very same Chinese text can be understood by two readers who speak two mutually unintelligible dialects. If one of them were to read the text aloud, the other would not understand him. Yet each reader would obtain the same meaning from the text, so long as each held a copy and read it silently. In such a situation, the ideographic system of writing has an advantage over a phonetic system in that it breaks down an otherwise insuperable barrier to communication.

Yet that advantage has been bought at a great cost. To learn even a few thousand characters of Chinese requires an immense expenditure of time and effort, as much time, perhaps, as it would cost to learn both a simpler, phonetic script *and* another person's dialect as well. Moreover, the very existence of so many splinter dialects in China can itself be blamed on the isolation of an ideographic script from the spoken language. For if the Chinese writing system had developed into a phonetic one, and if the dialect it represented had been taught over the whole nation, the result would have been to create a national language that was mutually intelligible to all Chinese citizens. But lacking an easily learned phonetic script, the dialect groups of China diverged further and further, according to the law of all spoken dialects— the law of change. Under those circumstances, even mass literacy could not guarantee oral communication among the Chinese people.

For this reason, the People's Republic of China has undertaken a vast educational project aimed at overcoming the disadvantages of the ideographic writing system. As the first step, all oral reading of the now simplified script is required to be vocalized in a single dialect—the Mandarin. Once this universal oral-written language has been taught to all members of the present generation, the next step will be "romanization," that is, the change from an ideographic to a phonetic (alphabetic) writing system. Considering the intensity of this effort, assisted by radio and television, the romanization of Chinese could be accomplished within the next twenty years.

This massive Chinese undertaking in the teaching of literacy could be judged a highly "artificial" intervention against the "natural" course of linguistic development. But the history of literacy elsewhere in the world leads to a very different conclusion. The past history of literacy in China has been the "artificial" element in the situation, whereas the present-day educational effort is directed towards the "natural" goal of literacy. For the usual pattern of writing systems is to pass from pictographic, to ideographic, thence to syllabic, and ultimately to alphabetic modes of representation. And the effect of this movement towards the phoneticization of writing has been in every case to stabilize and universalize the spoken language on a scale proportional to the teaching of literacy. The conservatism of Chinese culture, coupled with its religious conception of writing as inherently sacred (in contrast to India, where the oral tradition was sacred) may explain why writing failed to follow its natural evolution in China.

This conception of a natural evolution towards a phonetic script is the most important inference that I draw from the first category of research into writing. This developmental inference is almost universally accepted by students of the subject. Modern linguists as a group are reluctant to speak of "progress" in linguistic development, but those who have studied the history of writing systems have been unable to avoid the idea of progress as the governing idea of their inquiry. One student of the subject, David Diringer, self-consciously acknowledges this peril, presumably to disarm criticism by his fellow linguists:

> A word must be said about the "progressive" fallacy, of which so much has been written in other contexts. It is a fallacy inherent not only in modern liberal habits of thought, but, alas, in the very structure of our language and methodology of modern scholarship. Some would banish the word *progress* itself to the hinterlands: but *development* and *evolution* remain behind to plague them.[1]

Having shown his recognition of the problem, Diringer is free to state:

> All this is preliminary and cautionary. It is in no way a throwing up of hands or a denial that we can ever point to a straightforward example of progress in the history of writing. Such examples there have in fact been. . . . The appearance of systematic scripts, of which cuneiform was (so far as we know) the first, represented an immense stride forward in the history of mankind, more profound in its own way than the discovery of fire or the wheel.[2]

And in a later work, Diringer comes right out with the truth implicit in the history of the subject: "The alphabet is the last, the most highly developed, the most convenient and the most easily adaptable system of writing." This progressive view is shared by Marcel Cohen, I. J. Gelb, F. Fevrier, H. Jensen, and all other students of the subject, so far as I am aware.[3] Particularly interesting is Jensen's short chapter "The Universal Course of Development in Writing."[4]

1. D. Diringer, *Writing* (New York, 1962), pp. 16–17.
2. Ibid., p. 19.
3. Marcel Cohen, *L'écriture* (Paris, 1953); I. J. Gelb, *A Study of Writing* (Chicago, 1952); J. Fevrier, *Histoire de l'écriture* (Paris, 1959); H. Jensen, *Sign, Symbol, and Script* (New York, 1969); D. Diringer, *The Alphabet*, 3rd ed. rev. (London, 1968).
4. *Sign, Symbol, and Script*, pp. 50–53.

Turning now to research concerned with the semantics of writing, we discover a predictable limitation of scope to alphabetical scripts, mostly Western. Here, the historical and social influence of literacy has been the leading subject of inquiry, and the most recent full-scale study is that of the historian Cipolla, *Literacy and Development in the West*. To this may be added *Literacy in Traditional Societies*, with an especially interesting and valuable essay by Jack Goody and Ian Watt, "The Consequences of Literacy."[5]

As might be expected, works of this character are primarily concerned with the influence of literacy on social, political, technological, and intellectual change. To take a highly interesting example, it is suggested by Goody and Watt that the rise of skepticism and thence of scientific modes of thought was crucially influenced by the existence of written "histories" within a society. These recorded legends fixed a society's myth of its origins and thus prevented it from accommodating its sense of the past to its changed present. The resulting discordance between recorded tradition and present experience gave rise to a distrust of tradition in favor of actual experience.

For the purpose of this book, however, such fascinating historical topics must be rigorously ignored in favor of a linguistic consideration of written speech. For it is the linguistic peculiarity of writing which underlies the problem of composition. This may be deduced from the interesting fact that composition is a skill which must be taught or self-taught to persons who are well able to communicate in oral speech, and who can also read without difficulty. In addition, they have learned to form letters, to spell, and even to punctuate. Yet they cannot compose written discourse as effectively and communicatively as they can speak.

One explanation for the fact that persons must be taught how to compose in their own tongue is that they are less practiced in composition than in speaking and reading. That this is part of the explanation is too plausible to dispute. But it cannot be the whole explanation. Mere lack of practice in the writing of speech cannot explain the incommunicability of those texts which are formed when actual speech is transcribed. Anyone who reads a transcript of a conversation recorded by a hidden microphone will experience difficulty in grasping what the participants are effortlessly

5. C. Cipolla, *Literacy and Development in the West* (Harmondsworth, 1969); Jack Goody, ed., *Literacy in Traditional Societies* (Cambridge, England, 1968).

understanding (cf. the Nixon tapes). Moreover, anyone who has participated in a tape-recorded conference will have difficulty understanding even his own transcribed discourse. The fundamental reason that written discourse must be taught to competent native speakers is that writing is not "merely a way of recording language by means of visible marks," as Bloomfield asserted. Writing is a form of speech having its own special requirements.

Conceived from this special, functional point of view, only a handful of linguists have contributed to our understanding of the subject, and of these Henry Bradley easily towers over all the rest. Because Bradley had worked for many years as one of the chief editors of the great historical dictionary of English (the *NED*), his orientation to written language was more lexical than grammatical, but his emphasis on words did not seriously constrict his profound ideas on the subject. These he stated in a short monograph, simply and elegantly written, called *On the Relations between Spoken and Written Language with Special Reference to English.*[6] I shall briefly summarize what seem to me to be the most important points of that essay, as they bear on the functional relations of oral and written speech. I shall ignore Bradley's profoundly interesting remarks on the subject of spelling reform.

Although writing progressed from an ideographic to a phonetic system in all the modern European languages, these phonetic systems are not now *merely* phonetic in any of their modern forms (p. 3). From the fact that deaf-mutes can be taught to read and write alphabetic languages intelligibly (and also from other facts) we can infer that alphabetic writing is a separate and potentially an independent system of symbolization which could be used without reference to the spoken language (p. 4). Moreover, while the written languages of Europe were once primarily phonetic, they have now become, with the normalization of spelling and the spread of literacy, also somewhat *ideographic* in their function. That is to say, the forms of written words—their standardized spellings—have become ideographs which allow for a very rapid reading which proceeds at a pace faster than any vocalization of the written word (p. 9).

In addition, the modern written languages have also become ideographic in their *structure*, since distinctions now exist in the

6. Oxford, 1919. This monograph can be found also in Henry Bradley, *The Collected Papers of Henry Bradley* (Oxford, 1928).

written language where none exist in the spoken. This is the case, for instance, with capital letters, apostrophes, quotation marks, and such homophones as *sun-son*, *hair-hare*, etc. (p. 11). This ideographic structure in writing has allowed written language to develop on lines of its own, independently of oral speech. Its vocabulary for instance is far more extensive, so that some words of uncertain pronunciation exist only as a succession of letters, not of sounds. The essence of these words is their written form, and pronunciation of them is merely a symbol of that ideograph (p. 16). *Hence in these cases there is a reversal of the normal relation between oral and written speech. There, writing is the primary substance, and oral speech is derivative.*

Most important of all, the writing system of modern languages has determined in many instances the nature of oral speech even at the level of sound. By this Bradley does not mean simply that writing has tended to stabilize pronunciation (no doubt one of its most important influences on oral speech); he means also that writing has determined many sounds of oral speech. For instance, the adjective for Canada would be *kǽ nad ian* in oral speech, and "an illiterate person, or one who knew nothing but phonetic spelling, would be utterly unable to see any connection between" the adjective *Can ā′dian* and the proper name. "Yet anybody who can read sees at once how the adjective [is] formed and probably thinks the process quite natural" (p. 18). (This example could be questioned, since movable stress is characteristic of English.) Bradley's best examples of the dependence of oral speech on writing are outside the domain of proper names. If the normal spelling of *critic* had been *kritik*, the sound of the verb would have been *kritikized*, as indeed it perhaps should have been. The present form of the word has no connection with any phonetic law of the English language but only with the old graphic convention that "*c* stood for the sound *k* when final, but for the sound *s* when followed by the character *i*."

Bradley concludes with the observation that an alphabetic system which is partly ideographic fulfills the main purposes of written language far better than a purely phonetic system. He observes that many useful homophonic words continue to exist in literate speech only because of the ideographic character of writing. The word *son*, for instance, has disappeared in non-literate English dialects, while the word *daughter* survives. Moreover, without this ideographic function, the written language could not represent any large national language, since a purely phonetic script would require changes in spelling for very slight changes in regional accent—with chaotic results. In summary, Bradley's contribution to the functional study of alphabetic writing was to show (1) its *independence* as a symbolic system, (2) its *primacy* in certain respects over oral speech, and (3) (by implication) its *necessity* as the stabilized vehicle of a national language.

I believe it is fair to say that even the most interesting work on writing after Bradley can be seen as amplifications of his brilliant observations. Recently, in the work of Haugen, Householder, and some French scholars, Bradley's idea of the primacy of writing in modern languages has been revived, thereby reversing Bloomfield's doctrine in its dogmatic and universal form.[7] The most interesting statement in H. J. Udall's essay "Speech and Writing," for instance, is the following restatement of one of Bradley's points: "Although it is true that in the history of mankind generally, as far as we know it, speech preceded writing, it is not true that the present sound pattern preceded the present orthography."[8] Nonetheless, despite Bradley's intellectual dominance, homage should be paid to the work of Josef Vachek, a distinguished member of the Prague Circle, who has written more voluminously than any other scholar on the linguistic status of writing. Yet he would probably agree that his work is for the most part an amplification of Bradley's. For instance, the main point of his essay "Writing and Phonetic Transcription" is that "Writing is a system in its own right, adapted to fulfill its own specific functions which are quite different from the functions proper to a phonetic transcription." His rather more specialized but significant monograph *Written Language and Printed Language* treats a topic also taken up by H. B. Chaytor in the important book *From Script to Print*.[9] The germinal ideas of these books are to be found in Bradley's slender monograph.

7. E. Haugen, "Linguistics and Language Planning," in *Sociolinguistics*, ed. W. Bright (The Hague, 1966), p. 53; F. Householder, *Linguistic Speculations* (Cambridge, England, 1971) (Chapter 13 of this book is entitled "The Primacy of Writing," pp. 244–64); A. Valdman, "On the Primacy of Writing in French," *Modern Language Journal* (1966): 468–74.

8. H. J. Udall, "Speech and Writing," in *Readings in Linguistics II*, ed. E. Hamp, F. Householder, and R. Austerlitz (Chicago, 1966), p. 49.

9. J. Vacheck, "Writing and Phonetic Transcription," in *Readings in Linguistics II*, p. 157. See also the following works by J. Vacheck: *Written Language and Printed Language: Recueil Linguistique de Bratislava I* (Bratislava, 1948); "Zum Problem der geschriebene Sprache," *Travaux du cercle linguistique de*

The Context of Written Speech

The chief distinction between oral and written speech, when the two are considered from a functional point of view, is the absence, in writing, of a definite situational context. Oral speech normally takes place in an actual situation that provides abundant nonlinguistic clues to the speaker's intended meaning. Written speech, by contrast, must normally secure its meaning in some future time, in varied and unpredictable situations, and for the understanding of a varied and unpredictable audience. Admittedly, this functional distinction between speech and writing is a typical, not an absolute, one. Nonetheless, the important distinctive feature of written discourse and the chief difficulty of composition is its isolation from any particular situational context.

To illustrate this, it will be instructive to return momentarily to the transcript of the Nixon tapes and to consider their general character as oral speech presented in written form on the printed page. The transcripts are, of course, dialogic in form, but they are so unlike the literary representations of dialogue that, in contrast, even the most realistic-seeming literary dialogues must be recognized as artificial constructs. The Nixon transcripts' most striking feature is their frequent unintelligibility not only in nuance of implication but in plain sense. As the House Judiciary Committee discovered, the tapes had to be heard in order for the meaning of the transcribed words to be understood at all, and often the text was less communicative than even the worst student paper. Since the doubtful meanings could often be determined by listening to the tapes themselves, it would seem that intonation and timing provided essential clues that were lacking on the page. A still more important kind of clue required by the committee to supplement the mere transcript was the historical situation within which each conversation took place. From these

---

Prague 8 (1939); "Two Chapters on Written English," *Brno Studies in English* 1 (1959): 7–34. Also informative is the thoughtful work of Angus McIntosh, especially "The Analysis of Written Middle English," *Transactions of the Philological Society* (1956): 26–56, and "Graphology and Meaning," *Archivum Linguisticum* 13 (1961): 107–20. See also the interesting remarks of Vygotsky on the psychological relations between writing and "inner speech," in L. V. Vygotsky, *Thought and Language*, ed. and trans. E. Hanfmann and G. Vakar (Cambridge, Mass., 1962), pp. 98–100, and H. B. Chaytor, *From Script to Print* (Cambridge, Eng., 1945).

elementary observations about the Nixon tapes, the privative character of written discourse becomes obvious. Mere punctuation cannot supply as much information as tone of voice, and the bare text of transcribed speech does not normally announce its own situational context. It follows that writing must secure meaning by special techniques which are not normally required in oral speech.

Now it is true that these generalizations fail to hold in special cases. The typical differences between oral and written speech do not reside in the difference between the visual and phonic media themselves. Speech that is written down can be read aloud; it can be memorized, its script destroyed, and then spoken orally. A skillful public speaker can generate speech which requires no changes in wording when transcribed. Editors of the *Listener*, the magazine of the BBC, report that some interviews with highly articulate persons require little editing before their publication in print. No wonder! A radio broadcast is an oral equivalent of written discourse. The audience is unseen, its reactions unknown, and hence many requirements for communicative radio discourse are highly similar to the requirements of writing. It is not surprising, therefore, that the most articulate persons on the BBC have tended to be practiced writers, teachers, or public speakers who by profession communicate orally to an indeterminate audience in an indeterminate situation.

From the structure of these speech situations, it is evident that the distinctive features of written speech do not depend on its merely being written down. A radio talk is, functionally speaking, written discourse. A private note is, functionally, oral speech. Moreover, we encounter utterances which belong equally in the two functional categories, for instance, a rather formal conversation, or a very informal and elliptical letter to a close friend. As with most generic distinctions in speech, one discovers a continuum where one had hoped to discover definitive classifications. But a good reason for keeping the functional distinction between speech and writing is that the typical, privative character of written speech creates the main difficulties in teaching and learning composition.

The chief problem of written speech as a mode of communication is that a sufficient context for interpretation must be supplied in the absence of the many types of contextual clues found in ordinary speech. Written discourse has to make up for its lack of intonation, gesture, and facial expression—most of all, for its lack of tacit situational understanding and active feedback between speaker and listener. Transcribed oral speech seems puzzling and elliptical in print because the words alone supply insufficient clues to meaning. On the other side, a written style of oral discourse will seem extemely mannered—highly pedantic and roundabout—in ordinary conversation. This is not merely a question of "formal" vs. "informal" styles of speech but a question of what constitutes a sufficiency of context in two very different types of speech-situations. When people speak of a formal style of writing, they usually refer to those conventions of written speech which have evolved in order to create through the words of the text alone a sufficiently secure effect on an audience. This is the origin, for example, of the convention in writing that sentences shall normally be grammatically complete, with both an explicit subject and an explicit predicate. That convention is a very useful means for avoiding grammatical ambiguities in writing, but it is often unnecessary and roundabout in oral speech.

Conventions of Code and Audience

A functional rather than material distinction between speech and writing leads to the paradoxical conclusion that certain functions of writing must have existed in speech before writing was invented. For instance, a tribal chief might sometimes need to address his entire tribe—men, women, and children—on matters affecting the community as a whole. In doing so, he would no doubt employ the most nearly normative lexical and grammatical conventions of his language, and we now have evidence that such a normative dialect exists in nonliterate tribal communities of the present day.[10] This same tribal chief would also need to employ a style of discourse suitable to his relatively heterogeneous audience. He would need to compensate for differences of capacity and of temperament in conveying his meaning. He would have to speak with grammatical and lexical explicitness in order to avoid ambiguities, since he could not depend on feedback signals from a very small group. Naturally, his discourse would be monologic in character, and in general he would have to conform to the ever-demanding exigencies of making a speech. In every culture, the delivery of a monologue to a relatively heterogeneous audience requires similar techniques and conventions that are also

10. Householder, *Linguistic Speculations*, pp. 262–63.

found in writing. In all public speaking, one has to employ a "code" that partly resembles normal written speech.

The distinction between *elaborated* and *restricted* codes was introduced by Bernstein in 1962 and since that time has undergone a good deal of refinement under the influence of criticism and experimentation.[11] The empirical foundation of Bernstein's distinction (whether or not one accepts his sociological conclusions) makes his work a useful support to my speculations about the functional distinction of oral and written discourse. In my description just now of a tribal chief making a speech, I pointed out certain inherent communicative needs which required the speaker to use an "elaborated" code. Here is Bernstein's analysis of a similar situation in modern oral speech:

> The meanings now have to be made public to others who have not seen the film. The speech shows careful editing at both the grammatical and lexical levels; it is no longer context-tied. The meanings are explicit, elaborated, and individualized.... The burden of meaning inheres predominantly in the verbal channel. The experience of the listeners cannot be taken for granted.[12]

A restricted code, on the other hand, is the normal code for oral speech within a small group whose members *can* take a great deal for granted:

> Sapir, Malinowski, Firth, Vygotsky and Luria have all pointed out from different points of view that the closer the identification of speakers the greater the range of shared interests and the more probable that the speech will take a specific form. The range of syntactic alternatives is likely to be reduced and the lexis to be drawn from a narrow range.... The intent of the other person can be taken for granted as the speech is played out against a backdrop of common assumptions, common history, common interests. As a result, there is less need to raise meaning to the level of explicitness or elaboration.... Often the speech cannot be understood apart from the context, and the context cannot be read by those who do not share the history of the relationships.[13]

11. B. Bernstein, "Linguistic Codes, Hesitation Phenomena, and Intelligence," *Language and Speech* 5 (1962): 31–46.
12. "Social Class, Language, and Socialization," in *Language and Social Context*, ed. P. P. Giglioli (Harmondsworth, 1972) p. 166.
13. Ibid., p. 165.

The distinction drawn here by Bernstein may have a correlation with social class, for a number of extrinsic reasons, but the contrast between restricted and elaborated codes has no *necessary* correlation with social class, as the Nixon transcripts (conducted mainly in a restricted or context-tied code) securely demonstrate. On the other hand, Bernstein's linguistic *analysis* of the two sorts of code and his experimental basis for this analysis are sufficiently sound and memorable to be quoted at some length. Here is his description of an experiment conducted with middle-class and working-class children:

Consider the two following stories which Peter Hawkins, Assistant Research Officer in the Sociological Research Unit, University of London Institute of Education, constructed as a result of his analysis of the speech of middle-class and working-class five-year-old children. The children were given a series of four pictures which told a story and they were invited to tell the story. The first picture showed some boys playing football, in the second the ball goes through the window of a house, the third shows a woman looking out of the window and a man making an ominous gesture, and in the fourth the children are moving away. Here are the two stories:

1. Three boys are playing football and one boy kicks the ball and it goes through the window the ball breaks the window and the boys are looking at it and a man comes out and shouts at them because they've broken the window so they run away and then that lady looks out of her window and she tells the boys off.

2. They're playing football and he kicks it and it goes through there it breaks the window and they're looking at it and he comes out and shouts at them because they've broken it so they run away and then she looks out and she tells them off.

With the first story the reader does not have to have the four pictures which were used as the basis for the story, whereas in the case of the second story the reader would require the initial pictures in order to make sense of the story. The first story is free of the context which generated it, whereas the second story is much more closely tied to its context. As a result the meanings of the second story are implicit, whereas the meanings of the first story are explicit. It is not that the working-class children do not have in their passive vocabulary the vocabulary used by the middle-class children. Nor is it the case that the children differ in their tacit understanding of the linguistic rule system. Rather, what we have here are differences in the use of language arising out of a specific context. One child makes explicit the meanings which he is realizing through language for the person he is telling the story to, whereas the second child does not to the same extent. The first child takes very little for granted, whereas the second child takes a great deal for granted. Thus for the first child the task was seen as a context in which his meanings were required to be made explicit, whereas the task for the second child was not seen as a task which required such explication of meaning. ... We could say that the speech of the first child generated universalistic meanings in the sense that the meanings are freed from the context and so understandable by all. Whereas the speech of the second child generated particularistic meanings, in the sense that the meanings are closely tied to the context and would be only fully understood by others if they had access to the context which originally generated the speech. [14]

The analogy is striking between Bernstein's analysis of the two codes and my functional distinction between speech and writing. Especially telling is the contrast between speech that is "context-tied" and speech that is "context-free," the typical contrast that I have drawn between oral and written speech. That this contrast should have a correlation with economic class is not surprising, since middle-class children will normally be more intensively educated in reading and writing than working-class children and will tend to use a literate form of speech in completing a schoolroom sort of task. But surely it is their education in literacy, and their experience with a variety of speech partners that has made the difference, not money or family relationships per se. Moreover, Labov is undoubtedly right to extol the *superiority* of an elliptical, restricted code in those situations where it is normally used. [15] In intimate oral speech, a restricted code is the more efficient and trenchant form of communication. That the distinction between the codes has no necessary correlation with social class is further proved by examining any newspaper printed by and for a working-class ethnic group such as impoverished blacks or Puerto Ricans. These newspapers are always composed in an elaborated code and would of course be incomprehensible to their readers if written in a restricted code.

14. Ibid., pp. 167–68.
15. W. Labov, "The Logic of Nonstandard English," in Giglioli, *Language and Social Context*, p. 192.

The necessity of an elaborated code in such newspaper writing is dictated by the vagueness and heterogeneity of the potential audience to whom the writing is directed, no matter how narrowly restricted that audience might be in social class or in any other respect. Yet if the heterogeneity and vagueness of a potential audience were unlimited, writing could not securely communicate meanings which had any significant degree of complexity, refinement, or implicit feeling. Almost *everything* would need to be made explicit, and almost nothing, therefore, could be effectively conveyed to such an audience. Since effective writing always leaves a great deal unsaid, it must assume like oral speech a great deal about its audience. For instance, a written elaborated code can convey highly implicit meanings—including ironies that directly negate the explicit semantic surface of the writing. This could happen only if the response of the unknown, vague, and heterogeneous audience had been somehow brought under control.

In oral speech, that task of controlling responses is made much simpler for the speaker whenever his audience supplies him with feedback signals regarding their understanding and assent. The writer, having no access to such signals from his audience, is in an entirely different position. That is the main point of a very interesting article, "Logique et Rhétorique," by the philosopher Chaim Perelman. Perelman distinguishes two extreme types of speech situation—one where the audience consists of a single interlocutor and the other where the audience consists of "the whole of humanity":

> When it is a matter of obtaining the assent of a single person, one cannot in the nature of things utilize the same techniques of argumentation as before a big audience. With a single person you need to be assured at each step of your interlocutor's agreement, asking him questions and replying to his objections. . . . This is also the technique we use when we deliberate with ourselves. . . .
>
> The universal audience on the other hand has the distinctive character of never being really and presently existent, and thus of not being confined to the social and psychological conditions of a surrounding milieu. Rather, it is an ideal audience, a product of the author's imagination. [16]

16. C. Perelman, *Rhétorique et philosophie* (Paris, 1952), pp. 20–22. My translation.

Perelman's interesting contrast between the one-person audience of oral speech and the universal audience of written, philosophical discourse represents two extremes of oral and written speech. But even more interesting to me than this contrast between audiences is the realization which I gained from Perelman's essay of the imaginary character of the audience in *all* speech. [17] Every linguistic audience is imaginary insofar as the speaker must predict a probable response and a probable understood meaning *before* he speaks. (Everyone knows how easy it is to miscalculate the meaning that will be understood by even the most intimate interlocutor.) To speak or write is to project meaning as *understood* meaning, and this requires an implicit imagining of one's audience—a crucial point in composition teaching.

The other side of this imaginative projection of an audience in writing is the speaker's own imaginative projection of himself. While this may appear to be a wantonly paradoxical conception, it follows necessarily from the requirement of an imagined audience. If a speaker or writer needs to guess how his utterance will be understood, he cannot avoid the self-projection which is the corollary of that guess. For if his utterance is understood in a certain kind of way by his imagined audience, that must require *them* to imagine a certain kind of speaker aiming to convey that kind of meaning. And since that kind of guess by the audience is implicit in the speaker's projection of his meaning as understood by the audience, his projection of that audience must also include an imagined projection of himself as he will be construed by his audience. Speaking or writing is role-playing, as some sociolinguists and psychologists have observed, and it is so by the inherent requirements of a communicative use of language. That this double projection is often performed unconsciously in oral speech makes its conscious application to composition all the more important.

In recent years, these implicit speech roles have begun to receive attention from several quarters. Wayne Booth, for instance, has introduced to literary criticism the concept of an "implied author" as a necessary component of reading, and his concept forms a nice parallel to Perelman's idea of an "implied audience" as a necessary part of composing. [18] At least one student

17. See also Walter Ong, "The Writer's Audience Is Always a Fiction," *PMLA* 90 (1975).
18. See W. Booth, *The Rhetoric of Fiction* (Chicago, 1961), pp. 71–76.

of the subject has explicitly developed the global view that *both* imaginative projections inhere in both sides of the speech transaction. This writer is H. P. Grice, a philosopher.[19] Outside philosophical circles, his work has not received the recognition it deserves, perhaps because his writing is highly technical and complex. Still, his description of the doubly projective structure of speech acts has fundamental importance for all serious students of language use and all teachers of composition.

The generality of role-playing in speech, by means of these implicit imaginative projections, has a special importance to the craft of writing. In oral speech, a mistaken idea of a speaker's intention or of an auditor's response is constantly open to correction. But in writing, where these feedback signals are absent, the character of the implied author and of the implied reader must be more firmly and securely established within the verbal medium itself. Hence, just as an elaborated code is required for the "context-free" utterances of writing, in order to replace a situational context through verbal means, so, in writing, an inherent uncertainty about the implied author and implied audience must be compensated for by special conventions. All speech is conventional, of course, but writing is a difficult craft to learn partly because some of its conventions are different from those of oral speech.

Here I am not referring to the special scribal conventions of punctuation and spelling but to other kinds of writing conventions that enable a reader to narrow the meaning-possibilities of a text sufficiently for it to convey the direction and limits of its meaning. Beyond the general grammatical and lexical conventions, the reader also needs to know the further ground rules governing the text. That is why a single sentence in isolation is almost infinitely interpretable; it tells us so little about its implicit ground rules. Is this sentence from a dialogue or a treatise on logic? Are there implications of censure or irony? Such questions cannot normally be answered from a single sentence in isolation.

Hence, one of the important functions served by scribal conventions is to characterize the implied author and the implied audience and, by this means, to define semantic shape and scope. Mere explicitness, though greatly important in writing, cannot

19. See especially H. P. Grice, "Utterer's Meaning, Sentence Meaning, and Word Meaning," *Foundations of Language* 4 (1968): 225–42; also "Utterer's Meaning and Intentions," *Philosophical Review* 7 (1969): 147–77.

replace these further scribal conventions in serving this purpose. For, without an implied author and audience, no degree of explicitness—including the highly elaborate explicitness of legal writing—could suffice to secure meaning. Some shaping attitudes must always remain part of a tacit convention or guess. For instance, it is not usual practice *explicitly* to define one's own attitudes and one's imagined audience before launching into a written discourse. But even if one did this, the question would remain: What did the author imply by this disclosure? What are the probable attitudes of a writer who employs this device? Answers to these questions would still need to be guessed at, no matter how confessional and self-conscious the writing became. Hence, the implied author and the implied audience are never explicitly known—they always remain implied and unspoken. Their character must be guessed partly through tacit ground rules or conventions.

In writing, it is the normal convention for the implied author and audience to be semifictional and rather vague; semifictional because they both must be imaginatively projected rather than directly experienced, and rather vague because their character must be imaginatively available to a broad and heterogeneous audience. The author's inherent vagueness of personality, his semianonymity is, of course, a great variable in writing. Semi-anonymity is characteristic of Keats's poetry, for instance, since he was a poet about whose circumstances his projected contemporary audience could know very little. But the implied author in the poetry of a contemporary, Byron, is anything but anonymous or vague. In some of his poetry, Byron depended on the notoriety of his personality to project an implied author who was almost identical with the personality he projected to his intimate auditors and correspondents. A more recent example of such exploitation of personal notoriety in writing designed for a large, heterogeneous audience is found in the work of Norman Mailer.

But these are extreme cases. Keats is the norm. The writer generally cannot assume a very detailed knowledge of his likes and dislikes, his past history or personal circumstances. Similarly, the writer cannot possibly define very closely the character and attitudes of his reader. The reader, too, must remain only vaguely defined. Yet it is essential that *some* governing attitudes and assumptions be attributed to both of these imagined parties to discourse. Otherwise, writing could communicate only crude and uncertain meanings, which is not the case. We have at least one well-documented example of a text successfully written to be taken as ironical by one part of a large audience and as straightforward by the other part. This was Defoe's *The Shortest Way with the Dissenters*.[20] Obviously, the implied author was very different in the two interpretations, and of course so was the implied audience. It follows that, within certain vaguely defined limits, the implied author and implied audience *do* need to be established by convention and/or guess in order for successful communication to be achieved through writing.

How, then, are these tacit attitudes and roles achieved in written communication? On what conventions do we posit an appropriate kind of intention by an implied author and an appropriate response by an implied audience? The answer to this question involves a simple basic principle the application of which is indefinitely various: the convention that determines the implied author and reader is derived from the *kind* of text being written or read. Learning the conventions that apply to a particular kind of text is one of the difficulties of learning how to write and how to understand writing.[21] The conventions of the genre determine in large part the implied author's intentions and the implied reader's responses.

To sum up, the absence of actual persons, speaking in actual contexts, requires the creation of implied persons speaking in implied contexts. This eccentricity of written speech creates problems which cannot be solved by the ablest of native speakers without practice and instruction. That is why one needs to be *taught* composition in one's own language. That is also why effective prose was not born full-grown within the history of any language of which we possess records. First, the scribal, lexical, and syntactic conventions of a normative written dialect had to be established—the subject of Chapter 2. Next, stylistic solutions to the problem of writing effectively for a large readership had to be learned and gradually established. This process will be the subject of Chapter 3. Hidden within this historical process, traceable in all modern written languages, may be discovered the

---

20. A discussion of this example is found in E. D. Hirsch, Jr., "Current Issues in Theory of Interpretation," *The Journal of Religion* 55 (1975): 303–4.

21. Since these conventions are not definitely fixed, it may be misleading to stress genre rules in the teaching of writing. Probably, it is more useful to stress the need for giving sufficiently explicit clues about one's conventions, and the need for sticking to them once they are established.

underlying principles of composition. These principles, once established, may be codified; once they are codified, their rudimentary application can be taught and learned with ever greater efficiency, on the basis of research which, one dares to hope, will yield ever greater agreement on the nature and best application of these principles.

2

**The Normative Character of
Written Speech**

2 The Normative Character of Written Speech

For many readers of this book, a detailed defense of standard English as the proper language for composition teaching will seem too obvious to deserve a chapter to itself. Such readers may not be aware that recent attacks against this traditional view have confused and troubled many English teachers. In the present context, only a rather full discussion of the subject can suffice. A reader who needs no persuading on the point can simply skip this chapter, unless he finds the linguistic and historical aspects of the subject interesting in themselves.

The Conservative Influence of Written Speech

The universal law of every spoken dialect is change—obvious change in its phonetic and lexical character, of course, but also change in its grammatical structure. Some of the grammatical changes in English between the fourteenth and eighteenth centuries were dictated by phonetic shifts, others by foreign influence, yet whatever the various, complex causes of these grammatical changes, their inexorable tendency was to decrease the number of different inflections required to serve the same grammatical functions. Thus, in place of several morphemes denoting simple past tense, English was moving towards the universal d; in place of several forms denoting the plural, English was moving towards the universal s. This process of simplification still continues in every nonliterate oral English dialect in use today, and those oral uses which are now considered merely vulgar often represent a continuation of this historical direction in the language. This elementary fact, long known to historical linguists, produces rather startling similarities among oral English dialects that are quite far removed geographically. An early title of Eliot's *The Waste Land* was "He Do the Police in Different Voices," a phrase taken from a nonliterate British speaker in one of Dickens's novels. To many contemporary Americans, however, the sentence would appear to be in so-called "black English." The probable reason for such independent similarities in nonliterate dialects is very simple: the similarities reflect the ongoing process of grammatical regularization in English whereby the same functions will be always served by the same forms. Since the morpheme *s* denotes plural, and its absence singular, the tendency will be to regularize the application of the principle. Hence, in many oral dialects the paradigm may approximate total regularity:

I be		I do
You be		You do
He be	or	He, she, it do
We be		We do
You be		You do
They be		They do

Sometimes, the ambiguity in standard English of *you do* (sing.) and *you do* (plural) is removed by *youse* or *y'all* instead of by a pluralized verb. Because such disambiguation is functional, *youse* and *y'all* could both be considered an improvement over the standard plural form, as could the uniformity of the paradigms listed above. Such similar "deviations" within distant oral English dialects are, it would appear, instigated by an anomaly in the standard form which is removed by devices that are similar because they were already potently present in the language.

On the other hand, the far more powerful tendency of geographically distant oral dialects is to diverge ever farther from one another. Left to themselves, distant communities originally speaking the same dialect will, in the absence of any conservative influence, tend to speak mutually unintelligible languages after a passage of time. This was well known to Henry Sweet, the eminent phonetic theorist and the model for Shaw's character Henry Higgins. Sweet knew that isolated dialects tended to change the sounds of their words in very divergent ways, and he knew that these sound changes often had a profound influence on grammar as well as vocabulary. In 1877 he therefore made the following prediction:

> The result of these and similar sound changes will be that in another century any fixed scheme of spelling-reform adopted now will be nearly as unphonetic as our present Nomic spelling. It must also be remembered that by that time England, America and Australia will be speaking mutually unintelligible languages, owing to their independent changes of pronunciation.[1]

The century has now passed, and Sweet is proved to be a false prophet. Yet everything known about the history of languages during earlier times pointed inexorably to Sweet's prediction. It will be said that Sweet cannot be blamed for failing to foresee the advent of fast steamships and airplanes, much less of radio and satellite television. But these aids to rapid intercontinental communication are not the chief causes that have made his prediction false. Less than thirty years after Sweet's prediction, Henry Bradley made, in equal ignorance of airplanes, radio, and television, a prediction equally dogmatic and even more startling. In his classic little book, *The Making of English*, Bradley stated flatly that by the beginning of the nineteenth century, the grammar of English had become permanently fixed.[2] Bradley was fully aware that changes in pronunciation will affect the grammar of a language; that was a subject he had developed in previous pages of his book. So his prediction—going far beyond a mere century—implied a fixing of English sounds as well as of English grammar. Bradley has proved to be the better prophet. What did he know that Sweet did not?

From the standpoint of scholarship, very little. Bradley simply took into account a fact of modern life which Sweet, with his single-minded attention to oral speech, had ignored: the advent of mass literacy, mass education, mass publication. Under those conditions, if the grammar and the phonetic conventions of the national written language had become fixed, then the grammar and sounds of the national spoken language had become fixed as

1. H. Sweet, "The Principles of Spelling Reform" (1877). Reprinted in *The Indispensable Foundation*, ed. E. J. A. Henderson (London, 1971), p. 220.
2. H. Bradley, *The Making of English* (London, 1904). Revised edition edited by S. Potter (London, 1968), chap. 2.

well.[3] Even today, Bradley's confident assertion would seem astonishing to many a linguist. Yet nothing that has happened since the early nineteenth century, nor emphatically since 1904, when Bradley made his statement, has shown him to be wrong in any significant respect.

Some linguists of a liberal or naturalistic persuasion deplore the "artificial" conservatism which mass education has imposed on written and, by consequence, on spoken English. And almost every knowledgeable student of the subject concedes that some of the paradigms and spellings imposed by "prescriptive grammarians" of the seventeenth and eighteenth centuries were pedantic and unfortunate. But justice requires some argument in their defense. It is true that the now normalized English spellings, in British as well as American dictionaries, did not conform to pronunciation even at the time the spellings were adopted (*debt, enough,* etc.). On the other hand, the general structure and system of English spelling is far less chaotic than it is often supposed to be, a point that has been fully documented in Venezky's important little book *The Structure of English Orthography.*[4] But despite the defects of the spelling system as it stands, the advantages of any standard system—of any ortho-graphy—must, on impartial judgment, far overbalance these defects. For without a normalized, universal way of spelling words in the language, there could be no continuing connection between written and oral speech over all regions where the language is spoken. The alternative to a normalized orthography would be a more strictly phonetic spelling, constantly changing in different regions and ultimately creating those mutually unintelligible languages which Sweet predicted. A purely phonetic system of spelling for each region would lead to a babel as great, perhaps, as did the ideographic system in China.

3. "The 'making of English grammar' is now probably a finished process.... The ground for this belief lies partly in the spread of education. Literary culture perhaps on the whole conduces to tolerance of certain kinds of innovation in vocabulary, but with regard to grammar its tendency is strongly conservative.... We cannot assert that the evolution of new grammatical material—for instance of new auxiliary verbs—is altogether impossible, but the modern conservative instinct would render the acceptance of such novelties very difficult. On the whole, it is probable that the history of English grammar will for a very long time have few changes to record later than the nineteenth century" (Bradley, *The Making of English,* pp. 62–63).

4. R. L. Venezky, *The Structure of English Orthography* (The Hague, 1970).

The normalization of orthography was, therefore, just as important in the work of the maligned "prescriptive grammarians" as was their doctrine of "correctness." The grammarians were first of all educators; in Britain, in the seventeenth and eighteenth centuries, they took over the functions now served very consciously in developing countries by specialists in the honored field called "language planning." One such eminent specialist, Dr. Einar Haugen of Harvard, was some years ago summoned from America to Norway to help consolidate for that country a standard language and spelling such as the "prescriptive grammarians" had created in Great Britain. Nor can a national written language be formed without a normalized spelling. Although everyone agrees that the prescriptive orthographers of English could have performed their task more wisely, it is highly significant that no modern program of English spelling-reform has ever proved successful. Sweet himself wisely used the standard spelling for his publications. In this he showed himself more prudent than Melvil Dewey, of the Dewey Decimal System, who insisted on printing his preliminary essay in reformed spelling, making his work both ludicrously strange and difficult to read. Considering the great number of books now existing in present-day spelling, I see no reason to think that any thorough-going spelling reform will ever succeed. Nearly universal literacy will outvote any such misguided undertaking. Normalized spelling is one of the most striking examples of the linguistic conservatism which mass literacy has continued to impose.

Only slightly less obvious is the conservative influence of a standardized grammar and pronunciation on the written/spoken language. While one may again condemn prescriptive grammarians for supposing that any single dialect-grammar or dialect-pronunciation was inherently more "correct" than another at the time that the dialect base was chosen for writing, the same could not be said *after* the system had become established. The normalization of grammar and pronunciation is structurally equivalent to the normalization of spelling in any written language. It serves the same function of universal intelligibility within the community where the written language is used. Normalization of pronunciation and grammar is the indispensable foundation for mutual intelligibility.

It must be conceded that normalization has often been too strictly conceived. So-called "schoolmarm English" is less tolerant of intelligible phonetic, lexical, and grammatical variations than it sometimes needs to be, and fails to take account of the multiple usages appropriate to different genres and registers of speech. For instance, orthoepy—the teaching of a single "correct" form of pronunciation—has been carried to unnecessary extremes. [5] But the conservatism implied by such teaching, particularly when carried out with an intelligent recognition of the variations tolerated within the standard norms, is absolutely essential to the persistence of the written language as an intelligible oral medium. The following comment by Haugen is very much to the point:

> In the United States schools have taught the orthography and with it some kind of standard pronunciation as "correct." This teaching has unquestionably had considerable influence on American pronunciation, though linguists are inclined to discount "schoolmarm" English (while generally following it themselves quite closely). In the absence of a social elite, school teachers have felt called upon to exercise its linguistic functions in a democratic society. [6]

As Haugen implies, a strict association between the linguistic conservatism imposed by a normalized written language and the verbal conservatism of a social elite has been greatly overrated. While such an association may have determined the *origins* of the standard written language, the elitism of the written form entirely disappears with the advent of the little red schoolhouse. The primer is not a manifesto of social-elitism but rather its opposite—a manifesto of egalitarianism. That is the force of Haugen's historically correct observation. The American, Englishman, and Australian who, according to Sweet, would be unable to understand one another in 1977, can in fact do so through the good offices of the schoolmarm.

But the linguistically conservative influence of mass literacy does not extend to all domains of the written language. Intolerant of deviation in spelling, and fairly intolerant of deviations in grammar and pronunciation, written English in the era of mass literacy has nonetheless accepted significant lexical change. Actually, it has fostered lexical change. The written language has

5. An informed and judicious discussion of this matter may be found in M. A. K. Halliday, Angus McIntosh, and P. Strevens, *The Linguistic Sciences and Language Teaching* (London, 1964).

6. "Planning for a Standard Language in Modern Norway," *Anthropological Linguistics* 1 (1959): 18.

added to oral speech words and phrases which first appeared in print; indeed, print has been the agency of their promulgation. Literacy has also accepted useful lexical inventions which originated in oral speech. The schoolmarm may at first resist a word like *hopefully*, in the sense "it is to be hoped that," but not for very long if the word serves a purpose. Moreover, the many different genres of written speech permit an immense range of "nonstandard" or "incorrect" words to find their way into "standard" writing. The conservatism of written speech has therefore been the foundation of a genuine *lingua franca* within every large literate community in the world. The orthographic, grammatical, and phonological inflexibility of written speech has enhanced the efficiency and scale of its communicability, while its lexical tolerance has enlarged the semantic possibilities of the language.

The normalization of language serves to enlarge its range of communicability over space and time. In addition to providing norms, it also enlarges the range of expressible meanings by tolerating a range of variation from the norms. But no matter how we may judge the profit and loss, the advent of the printing press and of mass education has placed linguistic conservatism beyond the realm of mere choice and opinion. Linguistic conservatism in all the modern national languages probably belongs now to the sphere of historical inevitability. Probably, it is a force beyond the power of any group—of any government—successfully to oppose.

Recent Opposition to Normative Principles

The study of oral languages in the twentieth century has demonstrated that oral speech (when uncontaminated by the influences of literacy) follows linguistic rules which are no less rigorous than those of any literate language. To assert, therefore, that any oral dialect is "incorrect" is to state a linguistic prejudice which has no foundation in linguistic fact. Every dialect follows its own rules, and every competent native speaker of the dialect speaks it correctly. Correctness is an internal feature of a particular dialect, not an arbitrary standard which exists outside of the dialect. In its own terms, any variety of Creole English, any variety of regional class speech, is as correct as the writing of Dr. Johnson.

This doctrine of universal correctness, when stated as I have just put it, is descriptively accurate and logically unassailable. Indeed the statement is very nearly a logical truism; the linguistic conventions shared by a speech community are what they are. When those conventions are formulated as rules, these show themselves to be just as normative for that dialect as are any grammars of literary Latin, French, German, or English. So long as correctness is conceived to be a normative property within a dialect (and no other view of correctness would be scientifically tenable), then it must be true to say, as almost every modern linguist does say, that all dialects are equally correct.

This liberating insight, which freed modern linguistics from the constrictions of social and literary prejudices, has undoubtedly fostered some of the most important recent advances in our knowledge of actual languages. Yet it is fair to say that the misuse and vulgarization of this insight has sown error and confusion among teachers of literacy. I shall provide just one example of such vulgarization, since I wish to avoid, where possible, polemics which distract from the issues that are paramount in the teaching of literacy. But it is impossible to avoid mentioning the widespread misapplication of the doctrine of universal correctness, which has led to misguided experiments in teaching students to read and write oral dialects, as well as to misguided manifestoes with titles like "Students' Right to Their Own Language."[7]

The proper version of universal linguistic correctness is that each dialect is correct in its own terms and that any other test of correctness is arbitrary and erroneous. The vulgarization of the doctrine begins with the following process of reasoning. Linguistic science has shown that all dialects are equally correct. Students of language have also observed that all dialects serve equally well the purposes for which they are employed in a speech community and are all capable of adapting themselves to new communicative purposes in the speech community.[8] Hence, the foundational assumption of modern linguistic science is that of the *linguistic equality* of all dialects.

By this process of reasoning, the true doctrine that all dialects

7. This is the title of a report issued by a committee of the Conference on College Composition and Communication. It was published in *College Composition and Communication* 25 (1974) as a special number. A careful reading of the actual document discloses that its exposition is more moderate than its title. But, as one might expect, its title has been more influential than its exposition.

8. For a critique of this dogma, see Dell Hymes, "Speech and Language: On the Origins and Foundations of Inequality among Speakers," *Daedalus* 102 (1973): 59–85.

are equally correct in their own terms turns into the far from obvious doctrine that all dialects are "linguistically" equal. This further assumption is often stated as an indispensable working principle in scientific linguistics—one that frees the observer from linguistic prejudice and permits him a scientific neutrality. Yet the assumption is by no means a neutral one, and it by no means follows logically from the doctrine of equal correctness. Equal correctness establishes itself by defining the grounds on which equality is asserted, namely, correctness viewed as internal, rule-governed grammaticality. But dialect equality is an extremely vague, pious-seeming doctrine which can be sanctioned by linguistic evidence only if we are given the *criteria* on which one dialect is equal to another. By semantic slippage, a sound doctrine has been vulgarized into one that is either meaningless or untrue.

It is a doctrine, moreover, that subverts the very scientific neutrality that it was conceived to protect. To state that all dialects are equal is not to withhold a value judgment but to pronounce one. When evaluating two dialects on some criterion or other, one could judge that A is superior to B, that A is inferior to B, or that A and B are equal. To suppose that the last judgment is any more "neutral" than the former two is a delusion. Certainly, all three judgments could be made accurately without compromising scientific objectivity or expressing mere linguistic prejudice.

The semantic slippage and confusion which I have just described would not be worth attention in this book, if the well-intentioned doctrine of dialectal equality had not become widely accepted among educators as a firmly established linguistic truth. Nor would that fact even merit attention in the linguistics of literacy were it not for another incorrect doctrine about the status of normalized written speech. It has been asserted by some linguists of repute that such normalized written languages as French, Italian, Russian, German, and English are basically regional or class dialects. Modern written Italian, "as everybody knows" is the Tuscan dialect, elevated to a national status by the prestige of Dante and others. Modern English is upper-class London English fixed as the unique standard in the sixteenth, seventeenth, and eighteenth centuries, and so on. Since the normalized written language is just another dialect, and since all dialects are equal, it follows that *any* English oral dialect is in principle equal to the normalized written language. Therefore, to claim any linguistic superiority for the standard written dialect is to expose one's prejudice and to make a scientific mistake.

The linguistic mistake, however, is in the assertion that a long-established normalized written language such as Italian is basically the Tuscan dialect, in contrast, say to the Neapolitan or Venetian dialects. A national language such as Italian or English is not a dialect at all in the sense that the purely oral language of a speech community is a dialect. It is a different *kind* of language system, and the character of the difference may be grasped in the following observations of the Russian sociolinguist M. M. Guxman:

> One should not separate the formation of a written language from the activity of normative theoreticians, from the creation of normative grammars and first dictionaries, or from the activity of language societies, academies, etc. The negative sides of this normalization in the history of individual languages are widely known.... The normalization of the language in 16- and 17th-century Italy or France was of interest, undoubtedly, to a relatively narrow social stratum. However ... the formation of a new type of written language ... is impossible without conscious normalization, without theoretical comprehension of the norm, and codification of definite rules of pronunciation, usage, and inflection.... As material taken from the histories of various languages shows, the formation process of the written norm of a national language is so complex, the regularities of the process so specific in contrast to the life of a regional dialect ... *that the written norm is never in fact the simple codification of a system of dialect characteristics of any one region....* Under all circumstances the written norm of the national language is always the result of a certain isolation from its dialect base.... Not only do marked dialect elements remain foreign to it, ... but in the written language itself, vocabulary layers are created, and syntactic peculiarities developed, which never existed in the dialect base.[9]

Guxman's researches into the universal characteristics of national written languages should put in a new light the recent derogation of scribal normative pretensions. If it is true that all dialects are equally normative in their own terms, it is also true

9. M. M. Guxman, "Some General Regularities in the Formation and Development of National Languages," in *Readings in the Sociology of Language*, ed. J. A. Fishman (The Hague, 1968), pp. 773–76. My italics.

that a consciously contrived and widely promulgated national written language is normative in a quite different sense. The assertion that such a national language is a class language is shown to be factually untrue. (Had it been true, Marxist linguists like Guxman and his colleagues would not have hesitated to so inform us, instead of providing us, as they do, with ample evidence of its falsity.) The normative character of a national written language lies in its very isolation from class and region. It is transdialectal in character, an artificial construct that belongs to no group or place in particular, though of course it has greatest currency among those who have been most intensively trained in its use. Because of its historical and structural distinction from any dialect, a national written language has been called by Haugen and others a *grapholect*.[10] This terminological distinction, representing a linguistic distinction of great importance, can serve a useful purpose in clarifying ideological debates over the teaching of literacy.

A grapholect is a normative language in ways that cannot be attributed to any dialect. As a transdialectal construct, its *grammatical* conventions represent norms that are not only more certainly fixed than those of a dialect but are also more widely promulgated than the grammatical norms of any dialect. Its *phonological* norms are also, relative to any dialect, more certainly fixed and widely promulgated. A grapholect is the only repository of a large number of *lexical resources*, whose extensiveness is always far greater than those of any dialect. Finally, a grapholect serves as a norm by virtue of its actual or potential *stability through time*. Any long-existing grapholect has already proved itself to be a more stable, hence more traditional, language than any dialect. Even newly formed grapholects of the newly formed nations take on this temporal-normative character by virtue of their potential stability through time. If, therefore, one did wish to inquire about the relative "correctness" of two grammatical or phonological usages it would be at least a meaningful statement to say that the norm of *transdialectal* correctness is to be found only in the grapholect. But since correctness is more properly a criterion applied within language systems rather than between them, the more accurate inference

10. E. Haugen, "Linguistics and Language Planning," in *Sociolinguistics*, ed. W. Bright (The Hague, 1966): 50–71.

would be that among diverse dialects the transcendent norm of speech is that of the grapholect.

These purely descriptive considerations place in historical perspective the current debate over the merits and demerits of "bidialectism" in the teaching of literacy.[11] The term "bidialectism" is a nondescriptive, hence illegitimate, term when one of the two "dialects" is a grapholect. No matter how offensive sociolinguistic intervention may seem to some parties to the debate, and no matter how harmful tactless instruction in literacy may actually be, the normative status of a grapholect is an historical-linguistic fact which no ideology can overcome or evade. Once a grapholect has become established, it is as fruitless to resist its conservative and normative power as to tilt at windmills or battle the sea. Even energetic campaigns of modest spelling reform in English have been futile. To campaign for the more ambitious goal of reducing the grammatical and lexical norms of a grapholect to those of just another dialect, is not only futile but misconceived.

That psychological harm may be done in teaching a grapholect is all too probable, especially if the student's oral dialect is denounced as "incorrect" or "substandard." This is a linguistic error as great, no doubt, as the supposition that a grapholect is merely a class dialect. But surely the correction of one linguistic error does not require the commission of another that is equally great. What is called for is personal tact and linguistic sophistication. Merely to be a teacher of literacy is already to be committed to linguistic social engineering, and, while such intervention can be harmful, its potential for good includes the benefit of instruction in a classless, transdialectal instrument for communication between social and regional groups. To this may be added the benefit of communicating with the dead and the yet unborn. When a child of ten can read, with at least verbal comprehension, *Gulliver's Travels*, a book over two hundred years old, the conservative and normative power of the grapholect transcends class, time, and place. The teacher of literacy provides students with an instrument of communicability on a national and even international scale. All the great international grapholects break down barriers between social and regional groups. Just as writing

11. A characteristic polemic is J. Sledd, "Doublespeak: Dialectology in the Service of Big Brother," *College English* 33 (1972): 439–56.

itself was an invention which overcame space and time, so the advent of mass literacy is a modern innovation which has the potential, among many other things, to reduce the isolation and subjugation of every individual and group. Without a normative grapholect, a classless society could not be plausibly imagined.

Normalized Language:
Profit and Loss

The dreary uniformity of everyone speaking and writing in the same way is to many teachers of literacy a prospect which causes them to worry that their professional enterprise may deprive their students of cultural and personal individuality. These legitimate anxieties have created contradictory impulses in the classroom and in the textbooks devoted to composition. On the one side, the instructor has the duty of teaching the standard language; on the other, he wishes to preserve the individuality and expressiveness of those variations from the norm which lend personality and individuality to speech and writing. This second consideration has become for some teachers their paramount goal of instruction, even in the lower grades, so that "self-expression" and "self-development" are sometimes stated to be the chief goals in "language arts" courses. So long as self-expression is seen to consist in a variation of normalized language, no conflict of pedagogical goals necessarily arises in literacy courses. A conflict of aims does arise when individuality is expressed through nonnormative usage. Few sensible teachers will encourage this kind of deviation any more than they will encourage individualistic and "expressive" spelling. But the borderline is hazy and the problem is real.

No more striking example of modern anomie can be found than that of a completely normalized oral speech which betrays no regional or personal peculiarities. In recent years, even the BBC has ceased training its broadcasters in the deracinated BBC accent, and has encouraged a degree of regional phonological variation which it would have abjured ten years ago. Still, the range of BBC tolerance is limited. Pronunciation must still be "correct," that is, a variation not a deviation, and must of course be readily understood by all listeners.

On this delicate subject of self-expression, it is important to identify the genuine issues at stake. While it is true that a regional/class dialect or a regional pronunciation of the grapholect does lend a special flavor to speech, it is also true that individuality may be nurtured within the confines of a dialect as well as within those of a grapholect. Moreover, the range of variations tolerated within a dialect is always narrower than the range tolerated within a national language. Hence, the problem of individual self-expression is rather less difficult in grapholectic speech than in dialectic speech. The problem for the teacher of literacy is the degree to which he will encourage deviations based on dialectal rather than individual speech patterns.

The long persistence of genuine dialects in the modern world is highly to be doubted. Most of the evidence we have points to the gradual eradication of purely oral dialects. The process is a Vergilian one—*lacrimae rerum*—the grand imperium of the national written language gradually absorbing and effacing all local color, except in those unusual circumstances where a dialect is itself preserved in a literary tradition as a grapholect within the larger grapholect. Even then, the persistence of dialects is very much in doubt.

A case study of this gradual process was reported in 1959 by W. F. Leopold, a student of German dialects. These dialects were of special interest because the German dialects have tended to be more persistently spoken than the oral dialects of Western Europe generally. Leopold's report is made all the more poignant and telling by the unexpectedness of his findings: "My own observations gave me an overall view of developments in many dialect areas, the strong impression that the dialects were receding at a surprisingly fast rate before the standard language, ... and the conviction that the strengthening of the standard language is the most important linguistic development in German-speaking lands today. I had not expected to find this as the salient feature of recent German. My surprise provided the impetus for this report."[12]

This same process is likely to be going on, for instance, among the so-called black dialects of the United States, despite the recent self-conscious resistance to such standardization of speech. My own very meager observations of this process parallel the following, analogous ones made by Leopold:

Not long ago children liked to relax from school discipline by reverting to the unconstrained easy speech of the locality.

12. W. F. Leopold, "The Decline of German Dialects," in *Readings in the Sociology of Language*, ed. J. A. Fishman (The Hague, 1968), p. 360.

Emotional values favored dialect, at least for children from families that did not cultivate High German [the standard language] at home. Even where they did, but High German was not yet completely natural, the speech of play would tend to emphasize features which were not favored by the home, to symbolize escape from restraint. It is striking to hear children in the street, all over the German-speaking lands, now use more or less pure standard German among themselves, when the observer who remembers former conditions expects to hear dialect.... The whole process ... promises to progress rapidly with the change of generations. Children are ahead of their elders in the switch to the standard language. They contribute powerfully to the strengthening of the standard and to the decline of the dialects.[13]

Children have always been the principal agents of language change, hence, in the past, of dialectal divergences. Social linguists have recently established that children tend to favor the language of their peer group over that of their parents, so that with the widespread use of standard language on television, and with the continual movement of families in the technically advanced countries, it is more and more likely that the peer-group language of children will approximate the grapholectic standard more than does the speech of their parents.[14] If the children's peer group is heterogeneous in class and culture, the preservation of parents' speech is all the more precarious, and likely to give way to the grapholectic standard language in every country of the modern world where these conditions exist.

Moreover, grapholectic English can swallow and digest almost any lexical resource, and I am told this is true even in present-day French, despite the Académie. The national grapholects tend to be intolerant only of grammatical and orthographic deviations, while lexical items are allowed to come and go on Darwinian principles. If these lexical items are useful, and used, they are propagated and they survive. Some lexical resources of dialects are preserved, despite the imperialistic advance of normalized speech in the modern world.

But it is useless to pretend that all is for the best in this inexorable process of normalization. The distinctiveness of regional and class speech has more than an aesthetic or sentimental

13. Ibid., pp. 361–62, 363.
14. H. Gans, *The Urban Villagers: Group and Class in the Life of Italian Americans* (Glencoe, Ill., 1962), chap. 3, "The Peer Group Society."

appeal. It represents also a group solidarity which probably fills important psychological needs that cannot be met in normalized grapholectic speech. Whether or not such small-group solidarity will continue to express itself in dialectal speech depends on supralinguistic forces which control the actual persistence of the socio-regional groups. Increasingly, the movement of people, the standardization imposed by national government and national industry are tending to normalize not only language but experience. In the United States, except in stable and isolated rural areas, this normalization of social-regional groups is a fact of life, not merely of language. The anomie induced by large, heterogeneous groupings of people is not the result of speech normalization. Rather, social heterogeneity has speeded up the normalizing process to fill a need. In contemporary circumstances, normalized speech reduces anomie, rather than causes it, by lending people a means of communication with each other.

Therefore, without in the least discounting the losses incurred by the gradual disappearance of small-group dialects, I find the conclusion inescapable that the benefits are greater than the costs. This has also been the value judgment of some of the most learned and humane students of language, including Sapir and Jespersen. Since Jespersen is to be a guiding presence in the next chapter, it will be appropriate to end this one by quoting his brave and unhesitant remarks on the disappearance of linguistic species:

> If I am talking to one or two people, I can make myself understood best if I talk their own speech, but if I do not know their particular dialect, I succeed best by using the Standard Language.... The same thing holds if, when I write, I am addressing a circle of readers I do not know nor can see at a glance.... Nowadays no one can dispense with the written language: it is known or needs to be known by all. The question of the value of the common language becomes therefore identical with the question whether it is better that the Standard Language should be a foreign language to everyone, or everyone's most natural means of expression....
>
> Changes are always costly—the parents scarcely ever succeed in talking the Standard Language quite naturally, but the children can attain to it.... If the dialects are to be preserved by the side of the Common Language, it means that many will in fact be compelled to learn two languages, and those just of the class which is in other ways worst off and has least time for schooling. It will be more valuable for them to come into

constant and comprehensive touch with the Standard Language. They then acquire only one language and get a greater mastery of it. . . .

If we think out logically and bravely what is for the good of society, our view of language will lead us to the conclusion that it is our duty to work in the direction which natural evolution has already taken, i.e. towards the diffusion of the common language at the cost of local dialects.[15]

15. O. Jespersen, *Mankind, Nation, and Individual from a Linguistic Point of View* (London, 1946), pp. 69, 70, 71, 72.

3

**Progressive Tendencies in the
History of Language and of Prose**

Comparing the History of Language
and of Prose

This chapter must be somewhat speculative, since the history of prose is a rather undeveloped and controversial subject for all the major grapholects. It is a subject bristling with uncertainties and conceptual traps. I have chosen nonetheless to venture into this difficult terrain, because only an historical perspective on the subject of prose composition promises to yield principles which transcend historical and cultural contingencies. In the Introduction I asserted that the inherent ideology of literacy can be discovered in the history of literacy, and that the main goals of teaching composition are disclosed in certain irresistible tendencies of linguistic change. That assertion, while not securely provable, must now be defended as being very highly probable.

The abundant proliferation of different languages from a single earlier language, such as Indo-European, might indicate that language change is governed more by contingency than by universal principles. Students of linguistic history have proposed a number of models for describing the character of linguistic change. In the nineteenth century one popular model was the pattern of an early, gradually achieved perfection followed by a gradual decline: the Greek of the Periclean Age or the Latin of the Augustan Age marked a high point which was followed by slow degeneration. In the twentieth century, historical linguists have inclined to a more neutral mode of description which views any one stage of a language as being inherently equal, as a linguistic system, to any other stage in its history. Old English is neither better nor worse than modern English. This is the historical corollary to the doctrine of the equality of dialects. Other twentieth-century linguists, most notably Jespersen, and most recently Martinet, hold the view that language change is on the whole progressive.

This last view seems to me the correct one, though I must quickly state, as do all proponents of the progressive view, that language change is not progressive in every respect or in every instance. The respect in which the tendency of historical change has been forward is in its movement towards ever greater communicative functionality. This principle must, of course, be carefully qualified and defined, but once that is done the evidence seems to me irresistible that the languages of which we possess a continuous record have indeed moved on the whole towards increased communicative efficiency. If that is so, it would not be surprising to find that one special domain of language—prose—has also changed in the direction of greater communicative efficiency.

Jespersen first propounded his thesis about language change in an essay of 1891 called *Fremskridt i sproget,* expanded in English in 1894 as the full-scale study *Progress in Language.* He returned to the subject in the second half of his general work *Language* (1922), and once more in his monograph *Efficiency in Language Change* (1941).[1] In this last book, he summarized his thesis as follows: "In valuation of a language or a linguistic expression, both sides should be taken into consideration: the best is what with a minimum of effort on the part of the speaker produces a maximum of effect in the hearer."[2] According to Jespersen, the tendency of language change has been on the whole in this direction. In comparing the early and later stages of Indo-European languages one always finds increased functionality in the following points:

1. The forms are generally shorter, thus involving less muscular exertion and requiring less time for their enunciation.
2. There are not so many of them to burden the memory.
3. Their formation is much more regular.

1. O. Jespersen, *Progress in Language with Special Reference to English* (London, 1894); *Language: Its Nature, Development, and Origin* (London, 1922); *Efficiency in Language Change* (Copenhagen, 1941).
2. *Efficiency in Language Change,* p. 6.

4. Their syntactic use also presents fewer irregularities.
5. Their more analytic and abstract character renders possible
   a great many combinations and constructions which were
   formerly impossible.
6. The clumsy repetitions known under the name of concord
   have become superfluous.[3]

With particular respect to English grammar, Jespersen's view is
vigorously supported by Henry Bradley. Addressing the question
whether the changes in English since the days of King Alfred have
enhanced "the efficiency of the language as an instrument of
expression," Bradley states: "We have already pointed out the
great value of some of the additions which the language has made
to its grammatical resources during the last thousand years. But it
is not merely by the acquisition of new machinery that English
has gained in efficiency as a means of expression. The disappearance of superfluous inflections, and the reduction of those which
remain to mere consonantal suffixes, which in most instances do
not add a syllable, have greatly increased the capacity of the
language for vigorous condensation."[4]

Lest these opinions should seem merely impressionistic and
parochial, two points made by Jespersen should quickly be
introduced in their defense. First of all, since the tendency to
shorter forms and grammatical simplification is "a universal fact
of linguistic history," it is highly reasonable to conceive of
linguistic change as governed by a process of trial and error.[5]
Why should the most efficient forms of expression have arisen
full-blown from the start? It is inherently more probable that
they should have been slowly developed and codified. The
redundancies of concord (*virorum omnorum honorum*) originally
served a purpose in securing meaning, but if a way were
discovered for securing meaning without these redundancies,
then people would tend to adopt it and discard the redundancies.
This leads to Jespersen's second line of argument. The tendency to
greater linguistic efficiency is universal because mankind is
universally lazy and impatient. It is a human universal to
minimize time and effort in order to produce the same effect.[6]

3. *Language*, p. 364.
4. *The Making of English*, pp. 50–51.
5. See G. K. Zipf, "Relative Frequency as a Determinant of Phonetic
Change," *Harvard Studies in Classical Philology*, 40 (1929): 1–95. This was
Zipf's first description of his discovery.
6. This feature of language was placed in its larger context by G. K. Zipf in

The credibility of this last principle seems to me greatly enhanced by the fact that Zipf and Martinet have both reached the same conclusion, Martinet in apparent independence of Jespersen's prior argument.[7] Zipf, moreover, has assembled an impressive amount of statistical data from several languages to back up what he calls "The principle of Least Effort." Probably his most impressive data for this principle are those which establish beyond doubt an inverse relationship between linguistic complexity and frequency of use. The most-used words of a language tend to be its shortest words. When *television* is used often, it becomes *TV* (USA) or *telly* (Brit.). Martinet carries this point still further, applying principles derived from information theory and attaining a precision of measurement unavailable to Jespersen.[8]

Now if a language like English has grown more efficient "as an instrument of expression," it is reasonable to guess that English prose has also progressed in the same respect, since much of the corpus from which we deduce the history of English is its body of prose texts. And since prose is generally more representative of normal oral speech than is poetry, it is reasonable to guess that the history of prose must parallel the progressive history of the language as a whole. Although these are reasonable, almost self-evident conclusions, one must nonetheless concede that it is far more difficult to trace the history of prose in English or French or German than it is to trace the grammatical and lexical history of those languages.

This paradox is evident to anyone who has examined the work done in the two kinds of historical study. Whereas we have several authoritative accounts of the history of the English language, all of them in essential agreement, we lack, so far as I can discover, a single satisfactory account of the history of English prose. Scholars who have turned their attention to the subject disagree strikingly in their views on the nature and pattern of that history. R. W. Chambers finds continuity in the structure of English prose from earliest times, an opinion from

---

Human Behavior and the Principle of Least Effort (Cambridge, Mass., 1949), pp. 19–22. See also G. K. Zipf, *The Psychobiology of Language* (Cambridge, Mass., 1935).

7. A. Martinet, *A Functional View of Language* (Oxford, 1962); A. Martinet, *Economie des changements phonétiques* (Berne, 1955).

8. *A Functional View of Language*, pp. 135–47.

which Norman Davis vigorously dissents.[9] While scholars do agree that a shift in the direction of present-day prose occurred in the late seventeenth century, they do not agree on the precise nature of the shift or its causes.[10] And while early eighteenth-century prose often seems very like that of the present day, later writers of the nineteenth century sometimes seem more old-fashioned and difficult to a present-day reader than do some writers of the early eighteenth century. The history of prose style *appears* to form a wavy, uncertain pattern, unlike the more linear course of the English language as a whole.

The reason for scholarly disarray in the history of prose, as contrasted with scholarly orderliness in the history of the language, may be sought in the kinds of questions asked by the two different inquiries. The history of a language is a statistical overview; the history of prose style examines individual texts. The history of language normally asks rather precise questions about the disappearance of grammatical accidence, about changes in phonemic structure, and about the development of lexical resources. The history of prose normally asks imprecise questions about the relation of prose to conjectured oral speech patterns, about Ciceronian or Senecan styles, and about the use of rhetorical devices. The more rigorous studies of English prose style have concerned themselves with individual authors rather than with the historical pattern of prose taken as a whole.

I do not mean to imply that the history of prose would yield more satisfactory results if scholars asked better, more precise questions. The reasons for the uncertainties that beset the subject lie in the subject itself. An examination of prose writers from Thomas More to T. S. Eliot discloses anomalies and irregularities with regard to almost every trait of style. If one asked, for instance, how English prose changed in sentence length and word order, one could hardly make a single generalization which held without exception for every writer. To prove this point, one need only consult Visser's monumental, multivolumed *Historical Syntax of the English Language* and search in it for syntactic patterns which have disappeared between the sixteenth and twentieth

9. R. W. Chambers, "The Continuity of English Prose from Alfred to More and His School," in *Harpsfeld's Life of More*, ed. E. V. Hitchcock (London, 1932); N. Davis, "Styles in English Prose," *Actes du 8ᵉ Congrès de la Fédération Internationale des Langues et Littératures Modernes* (Liege, 1961).

10. A convenient collection of these controversies is S. Fish, ed., *Seventeenth Century Prose, Modern Essays in Criticism* (New York, 1971).

centuries or, conversely, which have arisen over that long period. I have not been able to find a single clear-cut example of such discontinuity—a result which at least suggests that syntactic deaths and births must be exceedingly rare over the past five centuries.[11]

Why this should be so can be inferred from comparing the prose of two very different writers from the same period—say the prose of Shakespeare and the prose of Ben Jonson. This has been done very ably by Jonas Barish, and what emerges from his comparison is the realization that adventurous writers will try out a very great number of syntactic techniques even if these are rare and strange.[12] Afterwards, the authority of such canonical writers as Jonson and Shakespeare will encourage later writers to use syntactic devices which may have become quite defunct in the oral speech of their own time. Similarly, the influence of a widely known early book like the Authorized Version of the Bible will encourage writers to use syntactic forms not normally found in oral speech. Hence, even if the historian of prose were to ask very precise questions about syntax, the corpus of prose works would yield an ambiguous answer to his questions. The interposition of self-conscious craft in writing makes the history of prose much more difficult to manage than the general history of language.

But under a broader, statistical conception, the contrast between the two kinds of inquiry is not inevitable. If the historian of prose allows himself the same Olympian view as the historian of language, he suffers fewer intellectual embarrassments. By and large, the history of language *is* the history of its prose, since most of that history antedates tape recorders and is recovered mainly from prose texts. Universally, in all the long-established grapholects, both the history of language and the history of prose progress towards greater regularity of syntax. Except in self-consciously individualistic writing, the number of frequently used syntactic patterns has become much reduced in modern times in all the grapholects of Europe. Except in the most contrived writing—which is statistically rare in any case—the scope for choice in word order has diminished since Shakespeare's day.

11. F. Th. Visser, *An Historical Syntax of the English Language* (Leiden, 1963–).

12. J. A. Barish, *Ben Jonson and the Language of Prose Comedy* (Cambridge, Mass., 1960). In Chapter 2, the author makes telling comparisons between the prose styles of Jonson and Shakespeare.

Recently it has been estimated that the total number of semantically probable lexical choices at any point in a modern English sentence—from the first word to the final period—averages out to ten.[13] This has been achieved in our language by the normalization of syntax. For us, the problem of effective prose composition is a great deal easier than it was for Shakespeare, at least at the level of the sentence. The history of language and of prose here coincide. Increased regularity of syntax, regardless of the system adopted, in itself makes language more efficient "as an instrument of expression" by reducing the range of expectancy and uncertainty both in the production and in the reception of speech. This normalization of syntax alone makes modern prose a more functional instrument than the prose of the past. To defend this assertion in absolute terms, as transcending cultural and historical bias, it will be necessary to ground it in certain absolutes of human psychology which transcend not only cultural eras but also the diverse types of human languages. Before turning to that complex subject, which goes to the heart of the composition problem in our own day, I shall discuss in a less technical way an example of the progressive tendency in prose from the sixteenth to the eighteenth century.

An Example of Progressive Tendencies in English Prose

Learning to write good prose is still difficult for almost everybody. I begin by assuming this undisputed fact of modern life, upon which a vast educational enterprise has been erected. I further assume that the difficulty of writing good prose arises very largely from the linguistic abnormality of addressing a monologue to an unseen and unknown audience. This difficulty, inherent in writing, I have discussed at some length in Chapter 1. From this fundamental difficulty, it is possible for common sense to make a number of predictions about the course followed by English prose, in total ignorance of its actual history. Moreover, we can predict a still greater number of historical probabilities if we add that the invention of printing made prose writing

13. "If you interupt a speaker at some randomly chosen instant, there will be, on the average, about ten words that form grammatical and meaningful continuations. Often only one word is admissible, and sometimes there are thousands, but on the average it works out to about ten." G. A. Miller, *The Psychology of Communication* (Harmondsworth, 1970), p. 82.

increasingly important for an increasingly large audience after the fifteenth century. On the basis of these elemental facts, it will be instructive to trace very briefly an imaginary history uncluttered by recalcitrant realities.

First, since every practitioner of a relatively new mode of communication has to start from already existing modes, we can guess that the sixteenth century post-Gutenberg writers of English prose took their chief models from two sources: from the prose of authors in other languages and from the oral techniques of public speakers whose monologic utterances before large audiences were necessarily governed by some of the same constraints and requirements which govern communication in writing. The misguided group of early prose writers who supposed their proper model to be ordinary conversation would have written less effectively than those authors who adopted the model of public oration.[14] Somewhere in the middle, on the standard of communicative effectiveness, would be those writers whose models came from prose in other languages.

Since the craft of writing for a large readership had not been widely practiced, the early sixteenth-century practitioners would need to invent special syntactic and lexical techniques which would help supply clues to meaning in the absence of an interpersonal context. Some of these inventions or experiments would prove to be effective, while others would fail, as experiments so often do. Gradually, these early writers would learn from one another, choosing those conventions which seemed to work well and neglecting those which worked badly. By this process of trial and error, syntactic and lexical devices would become gradually established, and, being established, they would then become normalized until one version of the device emerged as dominant. This subsequent regularization of writing conventions would in itself make the techniques more communicative than they were before the normalization occurred. For normalization in itself contributes greatly to communicative effectiveness.

I would conjecture that the prose of every country of Europe probably followed this general pattern of development between the sixteenth and eighteenth centuries. In every sixteenth-century

---

14. This is an inference that Barish draws in his discussion of Ben Jonson's attempt to be conversational; see his *Ben Jonson and the Language of Prose Comedy*, pp. 45–77.

grapholect of Europe, we will probably find great variations in the effectiveness of prose and great diversity in the syntactic and lexical devices on which sentences are built. By the eighteenth century, we should expect to find much more uniformity of practice. The more communicative techniques will have tended to expel the less effective ones, and those techniques which have predominated will also have become regularized. Any genre of prose in the eighteenth century will be found to be more uniform in style than a similar genre of the sixteenth century. The prose of the eighteenth century will also be communicatively more efficient. Since I have written down these conjectures in ignorance of the actual prose history of many European grapholects, my historical deduction a priori will gain much in credibility if my prediction turns out to be correct. No doubt I will find out after this book is published.

But surely no one will object that the pattern I have traced is incorrect for English prose. Let me give just one example for the sake of brevity, since I am not attempting here a documentary history of English prose. My example is formed by a simple experiment undertaken without any certainty that the results would support my general thesis. I decided to seek a work other than the Bible which, like the Bible, had been often translated into English. I decided to take the first two sentences of the first translation and follow their fortunes up through the eighteenth century in English translations. The work that occurred to me was *The Decameron,* and here are the first sentences from *The Decameron* published in English. They are found in Painter's *Palace of Pleasure* of 1566, a source book for some of Shakespeare's plots. Painter started with the third story of the first day in Boccaccio's original:[15]

> Saladin, whose valiance was so great that not only the same
> from base estate advanced him to be Sultan of Babylon, but
> also thereby he won diverse victories over the Saracen kings

15. To make the comparisons as fair as possible, I have normalized the spelling and punctuation of all three versions. The original Italian runs as follows: "Il Saladino, il valore del qual fu tanto che non solamente di picolo uomo il fe' di Babillonia Soldano, ma ancora molte vittorie sopra li re saracini e cristiani gli fece avere; avendo in diverse guerre e in grandissime sue magnificenze speso tutto il suo tesoro, e per alcuno accidente sopravvenutogli bisognandoli una buona quantita di danari, ne veggendo donde cosi prestamente come gli bisognavano avergli potesse; gli venne a memoria un ricco giudeo, il cui nome era Melchisedech, il quale prestava ad usura in Alessandria."

and christians; who through his manifold wars and magnificent triumphs, having expended all his treasure, and for the execution of one exploit lacking a great sum of money, knew not where to have the same so readily as he had occasion to employ it. At length he called to remembrance a rich Jew named Melchizedech, that lent out money for interest in Alexandria.

Here is the next published version (1620):

Saladin was a man so powerful and valiant, as not only his very valor made him Sultan of Babylon, and also gave him many signal victories over kings of the Saracens and of Christians likewise. Having in diverse wars and other magnificent employments of his own wasted all his treasure, and (by reason of some sudden accident happening to him) standing in need to use some great sum of money, yet not readily knowing where or how to procure it, he remembered a rich Jew named Melchizedech that lent out money to use or interest in the City of Alexandria.

And now the eighteenth-century contribution:

Saladin was so brave and great a man, that he had raised himself from an inconsiderable person to be Sultan of Babylon, and had gained many victories over both the Saracen and Christian princes. This monarch having in diverse wars and by many extraordinary expenses, run through all his treasure, some urgent occasion fell out that he wanted a large sum of money. Not knowing which way he might raise enough to answer his necessities, he at last called to mind a rich Jew of Alexandria named Melchizedech, who lent out money on interest.

As I shall mention when discussing the psycholinguistic testing of readability in prose, there are ways of making quite objective comparisons between passages like these, on the criterion of communicative efficiency. But I have introduced this illustrative comparison in the confidence that most readers of this book will not wish to undertake psychological experiments of a sophisticated kind requiring records of eye movements, elaborate control groups, trained technicians, and expensive equipment. Most readers will instead consult their own subjective experience of the passages—by no means a sure guide, but a useful one nonetheless, for grasping the progressive reduction of time and effort required to read the three passages. Also useful will be a very brief account of the syntactic-semantic bases for this progressive reduction of effort.

Justice requires us to exclude from consideration some of the lexical choices in Painter which history has rendered obsolete because of their marginal inefficiencies. We are not concerned at all to *condemn* Painter's style but merely to observe why some of his devices became obsolete by as early as 1620. For our purposes, the devices that are more crucial than lexical choices, or even verb forms, are the *syntactic* techniques in Painter. For instance, his phrase: *the same from base estate advanced him to be Sultan of Babylon* could be reordered in a variety of ways. It would be much more efficient to write: *from base estate, the same advanced him to be Sultan of Babylon*. That is because the altered syntax overcomes an ambiguity about the closeness of grammatical-semantic pairing in the original. There, an uncertainty exists whether *from base estate* attaches more closely to the subject or the verb. That ambiguity could of course, also be resolved in the other direction by placing the phrase on the other side: *the same advanced him from base estate to be Sultan of Babylon*. Moreover, the original placement of the phrase *from base estate* occasions another difficulty for the reader of English in any period; by separating the subject and verb and inserting a not-yet-resolved modification between them, the writer holds the reader in semantic-syntactic uncertainty for a longer time than in either of the above rewritten versions. These two principles—the speedy resolution of semantic-syntactic ambiguity and the speedy fulfillment of semantic-syntactic expectations— will prove to be central principles of readability.

The syntactic inefficiency in Painter is almost entirely absent in the version of 1620, where the imposition of effort on the reader is to be found mainly in the *length* of unresolved syntactic-semantic units. How the passage keeps the mind in a state of uncertainty is best seen in the second sentence, where three long participial clauses precede and modify the main clause. This arrangement requires a good deal of mental effort by the reader, who must hold in mind all these subject-modifications before their connection with the main clause becomes clear. In addition, one of the participial phrases is itself interrupted by its own participial modification: (*by reason of some sudden accident happening to him*). That this translation should be nonetheless fairly readable reflects a remarkable virtuosity in the translator, who makes the sentence work by introducing a tacit temporal and causal logic into the sequence. First Saladin wasted his treasure in war and magnificence; then a costly accident occurred; then he needed much money; then he knew not where to find the money; then he remembered a rich Jew. But this hidden temporal logic does not remove either the effort required by the long delay of the main clause or the effort required by subsidiary delays within the long participial clauses themselves. Most striking of all is the effort induced by the incomplete normalization in 1620 of special proleptic devices. Painter uses the proleptic device *not only* and then follows it with the now-conventional *but also*. However, the 1620 version introduces *not only*, then follows with *and also*, and follows it in turn with a redundant *likewise*. From this usage we can infer a still unsettled system of proleptic conventions, illustrated further by the now rare (in the sense used) *so powerful as*, rather than the more normal form used in both the sixteenth- and eighteenth-century versions: *so great that*.

Indeed, in the eighteenth-century version I cannot find a single proleptic device that fails to follow the present-day normalized conventions: *so-that; both-and; from-to;* plus a proleptic indication of temporal sequence—*at last*. Most important of all, nowhere in the eighteenth-century version is there a lengthy delay of syntactic-semantic resolution. The phrasing prepares and fulfills reader expectations by the use of both proleptic devices and parallel forms. Compare, for instance,

> *victories over the Saracen kings and christians*
> *victories over kings of the Saracens and Christians likewise*
> *victories over both the Saracen and Christian princes*

By the eighteenth century, even an anonymous translator has learned the trick of using the proleptic *both* to introduce a double qualification of a noun.

Further comparisons I will leave to the reader who cares to make them, for I wish to avoid the appearance of building a great edifice of generalization on a single example. Nor do I wish simply to multiply similar examples, all of which will (as I have discovered) lead to similar inferences. The common sense of the reader will foresee that further passages from the three translations of *The Decameron* will yield the same characteristic results. He might even foresee that a mannered translation of the late nineteenth century might be less readable than that of 1741, while very recent translations will be the briskest and easiest to read of all.

The great liability of examples such as successive translations of *The Decameron* is their apparent defenselessness against historical skepticism and linguistic egalitarianism. The historicist can quite reasonably object that the comparative readability of a translation will depend upon the linguistic expectations of readers, expectations which differ in different periods. To the historicist, only a sixteenth-century reader could judge the readability of sixteenth-century prose. On the other side, the linguistic egalitarian can reasonably object that communicative efficiency is an arbitrary criterion for judging prose. I shall outline answers to both objections before turning to the psycholinguistic principles of communicative efficiency.

My answer to the historicist is mainly to be found in the next section, where I discuss some psychological constants which operate in the human mind in all times and places. On the basis of these psychological universals it is possible to conduct tests on and make comparative inferences from texts written in different languages and taken from different eras.

My answer to the linguistic egalitarian must be less technical. The criteria by which one judges prose are not sanctioned by any absolute imperatives. The criteria have to be chosen according to one's purposes, values, or tastes. I am aware that the norm of communicative efficiency, even though it reflects the historical directions of oral and written speech, is not a norm that commends itself to everyone's taste. Nonetheless, a great many confusions might be avoided if I simply define communicative efficiency in a way that reflects its actual evolution in prose. Once that is done, I believe most persons will agree that the historical evolution of written speech has been in the right direction on the whole. Moreover, those who do not agree will find that resisting this historical tendency is quite fruitless in any case. Most people do prefer to achieve the same effect in the most economical way, with the least expenditure of effort.

A historically accurate definition of communicative efficiency will therefore lay great stress on the sameness of the communicative intentions being compared in two different texts. Sameness of intention was of course the reason for comparing successive translations of the same original in my example from *The Decameron.* And I have argued elsewhere in great detail the theoretical and empirical propriety of conceiving that two different texts can carry identical communicative intentions.[16] Those

16. E. D. Hirsch, Jr., "Stylistics and Synonymity," *Critical Inquiry* 1 (1975): 559–79; reprinted in E. D. Hirsch, Jr., *The Aims of Interpretation* (Chicago, 1976).

who dislike the word efficiency should realize that I use it relative to particular semantic intentions, not in an absolute sense. Prose meant to be admired for its ornateness would hardly be deemed communicatively efficient if it *were* highly efficient in an absolute sense.

This point about the relativity of readability is most strikingly evidenced in the prose of legal statutes. Their main communicative purpose is to make their semantic intentions understood with certainty rather than with ease. Sir Ernest Gowers, in his sensible guide to efficient prose, makes that observation quite elegantly:

> It is accordingly the duty of a draftsman of these authoritative texts to try to imagine every possible combination of circumstances to which his words might apply and every conceivable misinterpretation that might be put on them and to take precautions accordingly. He must avoid all graces, not be afraid of repetitions, or even identifying them by *aforesaids;* he must limit by definition words with a penumbra dangerously large, and amplify with a string of near-synonyms words with a penumbra dangerously small; he must eschew all pronouns when their antecedents might possibly be open to dispute, and generally avoid every potential grammatical ambiguity.... No one can expect pretty writing from anyone thus burdened.[17]

The criterion of efficiency is relative to the kind of writing being considered—more narrowly, to the particular semantic intentions of the writer. Hence the criterion can always be applied appropriately to any text. The decision to apply it must rest in part upon whether communicative efficiency names a question to which one desires an answer.

Psycholinguistic Constants in the History of Prose

The self-conscious creation of devices to increase the readability of prose would have been a rather low-priority goal of medieval authors. Before the wide dissemination of written speech in print, the decipherment of writing was a time-consuming puzzle no matter how excellent the writer's style. The medieval reader of a vernacular text could not quickly be sure from the mere figures on the manuscript just which word he confronted, so variable

17. E. Gowers, *The Complete Plain Words* (London, 1954), p. 9.

were the spellings of words in the vernacular languages. The reading process was slowed down still more by the well-attested habit of even the most highly literate persons in those days of muttering the sounds aloud to themselves.

In Grimmelshausen's *Simplicissimus* (Bk. 1, chap. 10), the hero informs us: "When I first saw him reading in the Bible, I could not imagine with whom he could be carrying on such a secret and, it seemed to me, solemn conversation. I saw very well the movements of his lips, and also heard his mutterings. But on the other hand, I neither saw nor heard anyone conversing with him." Chaytor adduces a good deal of evidence that this was the normal way of reading in antiquity and early Christianity.[18]

Only after reading became a preponderantly visual, and a potentially more rapid, process than muttered monologue, would the virtues of stylistic efficiency in prose have presented themselves urgently to the minds of authors and readers. Since reading habits were probably slow to change, it cannot be surprising that a difficult style remained fashionable well into the seventeenth century. In this connection, it is significant that the rise of utilitarian prose in the late seventeenth century coincided with the establishment of a normalized spelling—which is, of course, an absolute prerequisite for rapid visual reading.

Hence a tempting response to skepticism regarding the comparative historical study of prose is the response of common sense. When reading was very laborious, the decrease in labor effectable by style would have been marginal. When reading became easy through the uniformity and clarity of printed letters as well as through the uniformity of spelling and punctuating, the decrease in labor effectable by style became momentous. Prose style then became the only significant factor in the communicative efficiency of printed discourse.

Fortunately, we have still another response to skepticism regarding the comparative study of prose style in different historical eras. The psychology of communication, particularly as instanced in the work of George A. Miller, has yielded certain psycholinguistic universals which remain invariant in all times and places. These constants are based on two kinds of limitations in the human mind. First, we are limited in our ability to

18. The Grimmelshausen quotation (which I have translated) is taken from H. J. Chaytor, *From Script to Print*, 2d ed. (New York, 1967), p. 13. Chaytor gives further evidence on pages 13–21.

discriminate between more than about seven equally expected items in a sequence. Second, we cannot hold in our short-term memory more than about seven random units. Here is a comment of Miller's on the first sort of psychological constant:

> There seems to be some limitation built into us either by learning or by the design of our nervous system, a limit that keeps our channel capacity in this general range [four to ten categories]. On the basis of the present evidence, it seems safe to say that we possess a finite and rather small capacity for making such unidimensional judgments, and that this capacity does not vary a great deal from one simple sensory attribute to another.[19]

The universality of this human limitation is underscored by the evidence from both cultural and noncultural experience. For example, channel capacity is limited in about the same way for (1) tones of different pitch, (2) sounds of different loudness, (3) salt solutions of different strength, (4) points at different positions on a line, (5) squares of different sizes, (6) colors of different brightness, (7) pressure at different points on one's chest. In reading, if the disconnected items we need to discriminate are numerous, we will make mistakes in reading the phrase or sentence, and we will have to reread it until the items are regrouped into a smaller number of items.

Of still greater importance in this connection is the limitation imposed by short-term memory. Here again, the constants of the human mind are independent of cultural influence. It does not matter whether the items to be remembered are physical objects, binary digits, decimal digits, letters of the alphabet, letters plus digits, or monosyllabic words; in all these cases, people begin to make mistakes of memory when the number of items exceeds six or seven. If, in reading, we encounter a series of units which climbs above seven before being resolved in a definite pattern, we will not normally remember all the units held in suspension. We will have to go back to check up. And this will be true no matter what language we are reading, or what period we live in.

Of course, the matter is made exceedingly complicated by the fact that words are not necessarily the mnemonic units of prose.

A sequence of twenty-five words in a sentence is easier to recall than a sequence of twenty-five words taken haphazardly from

---

19. *The Psychology of Communication*, p. 31.

the dictionary. The sentence is easier because the words group themselves easily into familiar units. In terms of psychological units, a twenty-five word sentence is shorter than a sequence of twenty-five unrelated words. This means that the word is not the appropriate unit for measuring the psychological length of a sentence.[20]

The appropriate unit for judging the psychological length of phrases and sentences is the unit of semantic closure. As long as closure is suspended, the psychological length of prose approximates that of random words, though some word groups within that span may also be "unitized." For example, in the sentence I have just written, the first three words, *as long as,* are unitized. They constitute a word just as does *never the less.* In German, *as long as* would be written *solang*—a single word. Hence, the first four words of the sentence constitute two psychological units from the standpoint of short-term memory:

$$\overset{1}{As\ long\ as}\ /\ \overset{2}{closure.}$$

The historical skeptic can of course quite rightly object that the psychological units of discourse will vary a great deal in different times and cultures, and indeed there must be a large number of undecidable cases in making historical comparisons. But history itself suggests that the linguistic, unitizing abilities of a typical modern reader are more fully developed than those of a typical sixteenth-century reader. A practiced modern scholar can probably understand a printed Elizabethan text more rapidly than could a practiced reader of Elizabethan days. But such paradoxical conjectures are unnecessary. Actual, contemporary comparisons are themselves sufficiently persuasive, and the reader is again referred to Barish's comparison of the prose styles of Shakespeare and Jonson. Barish shows trenchantly why Shakespeare's more readable style, prefiguring the later evolution of prose, has commended itself to all subsequent periods. Shakespeare's prose fulfills expectations and quickly resolves syntactic groups. Jonson's style deliberately baffles expectations and makes the communicative error of modeling written discourse on oral conversation.[21] Those who complain today that Johnny can't write might be more tolerant of Johnny and his teachers if they recognized that the special demands of written speech are

20. Ibid., pp. 19–20.
21. *Ben Jonson and the Language of Prose Comedy,* pp. 45–77.

inherently difficult to grasp. Johnny can't write good prose for
many of the reasons Ben Jonson couldn't write good prose. The
most effective scribal norms had not been clearly established in
Jonson's day. And in our own day, Johnny's exposure mainly to
oral speech places him in a position analogous to that of many
sixteenth-century authors like Jonson, whose instincts for prose
happened to be less genial and prefigurative than those of Sidney
or Shakespeare.

On the other hand, Jonson *could* write poetry. Here are two of
Jonson's addresses to the reader—one in poetry, the other in
prose.

On the Portrait of Shakespeare:
To the Reader

This figure that thou here seest put,
It was for gentle Shakespeare cut,
Wherein the graver had a strife
With nature to out-do the life.
Oh could he but have drawn his wit
As well in brass as he has hit
His face—the print would then surpass
All that was ever writ in brass.
But since he cannot, reader, look
Not on his picture but his book.

I believe anyone can understand that elegant and gracious poem
more effortlessly than the following address to the reader which
prefaces Jonson's play *Sejanus:*

First, if it be objected that what I publish is no true poem in
the strict laws of time, I confess it; as also in the want of a
proper chorus, whose habit and moods are such and so difficult as not any whom I have seen since the ancients (no not
they who have most presently affected laws) have yet come
in the way of. Nor is it needful or almost possible in these our
times and to such auditors as commonly things are presented,
to observe the old state and splendor of dramatic poems with
preservation of any popular delight.

That passage does make good sense, as do all of Jonson's writings,
but to determine that sense requires proportionately more time
and effort from the reader than does the poem on Shakespeare.

A very similar contrast is observed between the poetry and
prose of Milton. Here are two beginnings—one from *Lycidas*
(1637), the other from *Areopagitica* (1644).

Lycidas

Yet once more, O ye laurels, and once more
Ye myrtles brown, with ivy never sere,
I come to pluck your berries harsh and crude,
And with forced fingers rude,
Shatter your leaves before the mellowing year.
Bitter constraint and sad occasion dear,
Compels me to disturb your season due;
For Lycidas is dead, dead ere his prime,
Young Lycidas, and hath not left his peer.
Who would not sing for Lycidas? he well knew
Himself to sing, and build the lofty rhyme.
He must not float upon his watery bier
Unwept, and welter to the parching wind,
Without the meed of some melodious tear.

Areopagitica

They who to states and governers of the Commonwealth
direct their speech, High Court of Parliament, or, wanting
such access in a private condition, write that which they foresee may advance the public good; I suppose them, as at the
beginning of no mean endeavor, not a little altered and moved
inwardly of what will be the censure; some with hope, others
with confidence of what they have to speak. And me perhaps
each of these dispositions, as the subject was whereon I en-
tered, may have at other times variously affected; and likely
might in these foremost expressions now also disclose which of
them swayed most, but that the very attempt of this address
thus made, and the thought of whom it hath recourse to, hath
got the power within me to a passion, far more welcome than
incidental to a preface.

Why should Jonson and Milton write prose that is less readable
than their poetry? It is improbable to argue that they *could* not
write readable prose; others, like Sidney and Shakespeare, and
even Chaucer, show that prose can approach poetry in readability during the earlier periods. But, without doubt, meter and
rhyme enhance readability for reasons which hark back to
Professor Miller's magic numbers. In pentameter and tetrameter
verse, the single verse-lines are short enough to be fully held in
short-term memory. In verse, the normal tendency is to achieve
some degree of syntactic-semantic closure within each individual
line, or at most within the space of two verse lines. In neither
poetic example quoted above is a resolution of syntax or of

meaning deferred very far beyond the space of two short lines. In addition to this quick fulfillment of syntactic-semantic expectations, the reader of the poetry experiences another sort of expectation-fulfillment which enhances both the onward movement of his mind and his sense of semantic closure. I mean meter and rhyme. The temporal falling into place of the verbal beats achieves a sense of closure even in the absence of fully explicit understanding. Metrical poetry has built-in expectation fulfillments absent in unrhythmical prose. That is one reason why many writers of the sixteenth and seventeenth centuries wrote poetry that is more readable than their prose. And since the contrast in such cases is between writings by the same authors, it is reasonable to argue that our judgments are untainted by anachronistic prejudices. In the eighteenth century, such contrasts between poetry and prose will become ever more difficult to draw. By then, prose will have caught up with poetry in readability. *The Spectator*, as Samuel Johnson recognized, represented a standard of relative readability which (English having become a normalized grapholect) could scarcely be improved upon.

In this chapter I have been concerned to suggest the irreversibility of this general evolution towards readability. I have cited the universal tendency of languages to move towards greater communicative efficiency, and have claimed that, on the large view, prose has also exhibited this evolutionary tendency. I have given some examples of this evolution, and I have referred to the psycholinguistic principles behind it. This historical progress was achieved primarily by developing prose conventions which set up ever more normalized patterns of expectation. Progress in readability also required a shortening of unresolved stretches of discourse, so that the reader could hold the words in short-term memory until he achieved some degree of semantic-syntactic closure. Now I shall take leave of historical speculation to examine how these psycholinguistic features still continue to determine the readability of prose, and provide in our own day an authentic foundation for the teaching of composition.

4   Refining the Concept of Readability

4   Refining the Concept of Readability

Efficiency of Communication as a Goal

Possibly the gravest misunderstanding to be expected from my readers will concern my advocacy of communicative efficiency in prose. Efficiency is a utilitarian goal that is apparently opposed to the aesthetic and expressive values of literature. If I now pause to explain again in greater detail just why my use of the words *efficiency* and *readability* are unopposed to aesthetic and other "nonutilitarian" values, I must ask the forbearance of those readers who have already grasped my point. I beg their patience on the grounds that a victory over this potential misconception is highly important to the practical usefulness of the book.

Ideological passions arise whenever one names any goal for the teaching of composition. Recently, Professor Lanham was moved to write a book-length attack on the traditional goal of clarity, and similar ideological confrontations emerged in discussions of composition at the Dartmouth conference of 1966, hindering a sense of common purpose among the conferees.[1] Probably my word *efficiency* is even less attractive than the word *clarity*, which implies to Lanham a conformity to lifeless norms at the expense of individuality. That charge against clarity may conceivably be justified, and I shall have more to say about clarity at the end of this chapter. But no such charge can properly be aimed

1. R. A. Lanham, *Style: An Anti-Textbook* (New Haven, 1974). For a report on the Dartmouth conference of 1966, see H. J. Muller, *The Uses of English* (New York, 1967).

at the goal of communicative efficiency, which means simply the most efficient communication of *any* semantic intention, whether it be conformist or individualistic. Some semantic intentions require prose that is complex and difficult to read. An attempt to express those intentions in easy-to-read prose would properly be condemned as inefficient writing. *Communicative efficiency* is synonymous with *relative readability*, and both imply the relativity of my criterion to the writer's semantic intentions. Some of the prose of William Faulkner is not very readable on an absolute scale, but many of these passages rank high in relative readability, since they are highly efficient in communicating Faulkner's complex semantic intentions.

Another potential misconception of efficiency can arise when the distinction between linguistic efficiency in oral speech and linguistic efficiency in prose is forgotten. The theory of progressive efficiency in language evolution was applied by Jespersen, Zipf, and Martinet to oral speech, and they agreed that the appraisal of efficiency had to take account of both sides of oral speech—the speaker's side as well as the listener's. What takes less effort to say might take more effort to understand, and vice versa. They found a net gain in efficiency for a particular meaning if the effort was less on both sides, or if the effort stayed the same on one side but was less on the other. By contrast, the appraisal of efficiency in prose is entirely one-sided—hence my equation of efficiency in prose with readability. For the reader, the longer way is often the faster way, and what is understood easily and rapidly by the reader may be the result of five or six painstaking revisions by the writer.

Implicit in this conception of readability is the *rhetorical* efficiency of prose—its success in affecting the implied reader in ways that transcend the mere conveying of information. Since that dimension of the writer's semantic intentions is an essential part of meaning in prose, it is also an essential consideration in any judgment of communicative efficiency.

Can this one-sided goal of efficiency, that is, relative readability, be defended on grounds which transcend not only personal preference but even historical evolution? The answer is "yes." In the previous chapter I clothed the criterion of readability with the mantle of historical inevitability. But this historical process can be resisted, and in fact was resisted by a number of authors in the Victorian age. Theirs was a misguided effort, as the majority of their Victorian contemporaries under-stood.[2] For, the goal of readability in prose implies values that are fundamental to all of speech. That this goal of communicative efficiency does not necessarily conflict with stylistic individuality, complexity, or elegance should now be sufficiently clear in principle, and I intend to devote the rest of this book mainly to the problem of achieving this pedagogical goal rather than to the problem of defending it.

An Early Discussion of Readability

In 1852 Herbert Spencer, displaying the acumen that later made him a leading thinker of his time, published an essay on prose in the *Westminster Review* entitled "The Philosophy of Style."[3] This essay, though not widely noticed in recent work, has never been superseded. In some of his observations Spencer was almost certainly wrong, but he was rarely wrong in the general principles he enunciated. Indeed, some of his genial hunches have been confirmed by very recent research in linguistics, psycho-linguistics, and psychology. This essay of Spencer's is, I believe, the best introduction to the subject of readability, and a good starting point for my discussion of the topic. Although Spencer did not himself use the word *readability*, he used the meaning, which he expressed in the phrases "economy of the reader's attention" and "least possible mental effort."

Spencer announced his goal to be the reduction of all rhetorical maxims to a single principle. "The maxims contained in works on composition and rhetoric are presented in an unorganized form. Standing as isolated dogmas—as empirical generalizations, they are neither so clearly apprehended, nor so much respected, as they would be were they deduced from some simple first principle." Spencer observed that if we look through the standard handbooks (he named works by Whateley, Kaimes, and Blair), we discover that the rules they present in isolation do in fact presuppose a common principle:

> On seeking for some clue to the law underlying these current
> maxims, we may see implied in many of them, the importance

2. The statistical norm for Victorian prose is found in popular newspapers and *My Secret Life*, not in Carlyle and Pater.

3. The essay was reprinted in Spencer's *Essays, Moral, Political and Aesthetic* (New York, 1868), and in subsequent anthologies.

of economizing the reader's or hearer's attention. To so present ideas that they may be apprehended with the least possible mental effort, is the desideratum towards which most of the rules above quoted point. When we condemn writing that is wordy or confused, or intricate—when we praise this style as easy, and blame that as fatiguing, we consciously or unconsciously assume this desideratum as our standard of judgment.

Behind Spencer's principle of least effort lay an assumption about the use of language which he quite explicitly announced: language is the "vehicle of thought," a means to an end rather than an end in itself. The aim is "to present ideas," to "express an idea." But Spencer's conception was a good deal richer than these phrases taken in isolation suggest, and the phrases are found early in the first part of his essay. The second part moves from a consideration of least effort to a consideration of greatest effect, and from "the economy of mental energies" to the "economy of the mental sensibilities." Here, in this second part, Spencer deals with the importance of stylistic variety for achieving interest, force, and delight. But these effects of variety are hardly ideas to be "carried" by a vehicle; they are the psychological effects of style and comprise both a semantic effect and an emotive or artistic effect. By introducing these further pyschological considerations, Spencer shows, without directly admitting it, that the principle of least effort is by itself an insufficient principle for composition. Other principles must be added besides the most efficient presentation of "thoughts."

His use of the single word "economy" to mean both *efficiency* of word order and *variety* of presentation was a lexical sleight-of-hand. These stylistic traits are not double aspects of a single principle; Spencer has really subsumed two principles under the single word *economy*. That is probably the gravest intellectual flaw in his brilliant essay, for this error in logic prevented him from stressing the need for constant compromises between several sometimes conflicting psychological principles of composition.[4] Hence, the first part of Spencer's essay will be more readily appreciated when we keep in mind his implicit recognition that meanings are something more than ideas, and relative readability something more than the principle of least effort.

4. Yet Spencer's conflation of economy and variety is justified in many cases. Monotony of style does increase the reader's effort. See D. E. Broadbent, *Perception and Communication* (Oxford, 1958), pp. 135–38.

Behind Spencer's emphasis on economizing the reader's attention was his correct intuition that the time and effort devoted to the decipherment of meaning would be subtracted from the energy left to consider the meaning itself. This perhaps obvious point has recently been confirmed in psychological experiments.[5] But the concept is obvious only after somebody has conceived it, and Spencer was, I believe, the first writer to suggest that a reader has, in current terms, a "limited channel-capacity":

> A reader or listener has at each moment but a limited amount of mental power available. To recognize and interpret the symbols presented to him requires part of this power; to arrange and combine the images suggested by them requires a further part; and only that part which remains can be used for framing the thought expressed. Hence the more time and attention it takes to receive and understand each sentence, the less time and attention can be given to the contained idea; and the less vividly will that idea be conceived.

This statement holds true only if we assume that a sentence is given but one perusal, since we *could* read the sentence, or some parts of it, twice or thrice, attending fully to the meaning after we have deciphered the sentence. In the next chapter I shall explain why a prose style requiring a second perusal is *never* justified if such a style can be avoided. Assuming for the moment that this claim is true, we can say that Spencer's assertion just quoted must also be true.

From the reader's limited channel-capacity, Spencer explains a number of stylistic rules which had existed before simply as unsupported dogmas. For instance, the asserted superiority in English of Saxon words over Latin words he deduced from the shortness of the Saxon: "If it be an advantage to express an idea in the smallest number of words, then it must be an advantage to express it in the smallest number of syllables." This doctrine seems self-evidently correct in cases where a short word performs the same semantic function as a long word, since in a given span of time, less time and effort would be required for pure decipherment, and hence more energy would be left to consider meaning. Yet Spencer quickly concedes that a short word cannot always serve the same semantic function as a long one, cannot, for instance, always yield the same force and emphasis. *Magnificent* is grander than *grand*, because it "allows the reader's conscious-

5. These results are discussed in the next chapter.

ness more time to dwell on the quality predicated." But usually the shorter word spares the reader both effort and time.

In fact, however, as Martinet has rightly argued, a shorter expression is not always easier for a reader.[6] While it is true that, other things being equal, a short expression costs the reader less energy than a long one, we know that other things are rarely equal. That is why Spencer sought still deeper reasons for normally preferring Saxon to Latin words in English composition. Doubtful as the maxim itself might be, Spencer's further explanation was profoundly accurate in the principle it enunciated. The most important reason for the low energy-cost of Saxon words is their greater familiarity through their greater frequency of use. "A child's vocabulary is almost wholly Saxon.... The synonyms learned in after years never become so closely, so organically connected with the ideas signified as do these original words used in childhood.... Increasing familiarity ... brings greater rapidity and ease of comprehension."

Spencer's explanation for the greater readability of Saxon words is thus a double explanation: they are shorter than Latin words and they are more familiar than Latin words. Their mere shortness is not a sufficient explanation of their low-energy cost. In this double explanation, Spencer has foreshadowed one of the epochal distinctions of modern linguistics—Saussure's distinction between the syntagmatic and the paradigmatic aspects of language use, a distinction which, in some form or other, is required to determine the actual psychic energy needed to interpret a stretch of written discourse.[7] Briefly, the syntagmatic relations of words consist in their temporal sequence:

$$\overset{1}{The}\ \overset{2}{cat}\ \overset{3}{is}\ \overset{4}{on}\ \overset{5}{the}\ \overset{6}{mat}.$$

But their paradigmatic relations, (which I shall illustrate below) though far more important, are quite invisible on the page. *The cat* (a domestic animal) is easier than *the cat* (a leopard) because the first inhabits a more usual and familiar paradigmatic domain; the first *cat* belongs to a paradigmatic domain (*dogs* and *cats*) more usual than the second domain (*cougars* and *leopards*, etc.). Moreover *cat* in both senses belongs to paradigmatic domains which are more familiar than that of *feline*. *Cat* is not

6. *A Functional View of Language*, p. 141.
7. F. de Saussure, *Course in General Linguistics*, (New York, 1959), pp. 122–27.

only shorter in itself than *feline,* it also requires a shorter time for semantic processing in the paradigmatic dimension.

But on the whole, Spencer's speculations limit themselves to the syntagmatic dimension, to the sequence of words in a sentence, and the sequence of sentences in a discourse. The best sequence for economizing the reader's attention is the sequence which leaves the reader in uncertainty for the shortest period of time: "As in a narrative, the events should be stated in such sequence that the mind may not have to go backwards and forwards in order to rightly connect them; as in a group of sentences, the arrangement should be such that each of them may be understood as it comes without waiting for subsequent ones; so in every sentence, the sequence of words should be that which suggests the constituents of thought in the order most convenient for building it up."

What considerations determine "the most convenient" order of words in a sentence? At times Spencer seems to imply that writers of a modern grapholect have much more syntactic choice than they actually do. His discussion of the superiority of English adjective placement over French is at once provincial and incorrect. (He argued that *a black horse* is inherently easier to understand than *a horse black;* while a Frenchman would certainly reply that *un noir cheval* is far harder to understand than *un cheval noir.* Both normal versions are quite identically economical in their native domains, for both stay within the bounds of short-term memory, a recent concept which Spencer could not have been expected to discover.) Spencer's more correct and profound comments about the most readable order of words are those which go beyond details like adjective placement and concern themselves with the larger syntactic relations within sentences.

His primary syntactic principle requires that "expressions which refer to the most nearly connected thoughts shall be brought the closest together." As stated, the principle sounds vague and unhelpful. How does one decide the closeness of thoughts? For instance, in Spencer's own sentence, just quoted, should he not have written: "expressions which refer to thoughts most nearly connected shall be brought the closest together." This rewriting brings *thoughts* closer to *refer,* yet leaves *most nearly connected* just as close to *thoughts* as before. In fact, other considerations make Spencer's original slightly easier, in my opinion. It is not Spencer's maxim that goes to the heart of the matter but rather his explanation, in which he describes the single most important factor in the syntactic dimension of readability:

> The longer the time that elapses between the mention of any qualifying member and the member qualified, the longer must the mind be exerted in carrying forward the qualifying member ready for use. And the more numerous the qualifications to be simultaneously remembered and rightly applied, the greater will be the mental power expended, and the smaller the effect produced. Hence, other things equal, force will be gained by so arranging the members of a sentence *that these suspensions shall at any moment be the fewest in number, and shall also be of the shortest duration.* [My italics]

The importance of this maxim can hardly be overrated. Spencer's example of a good use of the maxim shows his acumen and also nicely confirms a point about Milton's poetry made at the end of the previous chapter, for Spencer's example of good syntactic arrangement is taken from *Paradise Lost:*

> As when a prowling wolf,
> Whom hunger drives to seek new haunt for prey,
> Watching where shepherds pen their flocks at eve,
> In hurdled cotes amid the field secure,
> Leaps o'er the fence with ease into the fold:
> Or as a thief, bent to unhoard the cash
> Of some rich burgher, whose substantial doors,
> Cross-barr'd and bolted fast, fear no assault,
> In at the window climbs, or o'er the tiles:
> So clomb the first grand Thief into God's fold;
> So since into his church lewd hirelings climb.

Unquestionably, the syntactic-semantic suspensions of these lines are kept wonderfully brief, considering the intricacy and richness of the relationships expressed—relationships more intricate and rich than occur at the beginning of *Aeropagitica,* yet much more easily understood.

Indeed, in another context, Spencer commented upon the potential advantages of poetry over prose in terms rather similar to those in which I compared the poetry and prose of Milton: "Any mode of so combining words as to present a regular recurrence of certain traits which can be anticipated, will diminish that strain on the attention entailed by the total irregularity of prose.... If the syllables be rhythmically arranged, the mind may economize its energies by anticipating the attention required for each syllable.... If we habitually pre-adjust our perceptions to the measured movement of verse ... it is probable that by so doing we economize attention; and hence that metrical language is more effective than prose because it enables us to do this. Were there space, it might be worthwhile to inquire whether the pleasure we take in rhyme, and also that which we take in euphony, are not partly ascribable to the same general cause." Spencer's yoking of regularity in rhythm with the idea of "anticipation" and "pre-adjustment" in the mind is yet another genial stroke which suggests what will prove to be yet another crucial element in readability: the principle of expecta-tion-fullfillment.

Spencer ends his essay with a psychological explanation for the importance of variety in sentence style, his point being that the easiest style is not always the best if it is achieved at the cost of boredom or "fatigue." In this qualification of his principle, Spencer implicitly acknowledges its inherent relativity to autho-rial intentions. For there might very well be instances in which economy of reader effort is deemed more important than the probability of reader fatigue. In a technical manual on a difficult subject, an author might be unconcerned with the objection Spencer brought against the work of Alexander Pope—that it was *always* easy to read, and therefore fatiguing. But elsewhere, Spencer's qualification might be a decisive consideration for an author. This relativity in the principle of least effort is implicit in Spencer's repeated tag "other things equal." Other things equal, the easiest style is the best. In achieving the same semantic intentions, the easiest style is the best. In this essay, Spencer has adumbrated many key principles of readability, and (implicitly) the principle of *relative* readability as well.

Recent Research on Readability

Although the word *readability* conveys very well the idea of communicative efficiency in prose, it is tainted for some scholars by its almost exclusive association with testing the reading-difficulty of texts for young schoolchildren. This use of the word by educational psychologists since the 1930s has served very reasonable goals in primary education. The aim was to devise a simple, easily applied, and reliable formula for determining the reading difficulty of a text on an absolute scale. The result of applying such a formula would be to inform a publisher, teacher, or schoolboard whether the prose of a text was too difficult for a particular group of schoolchildren. Extended to other fields, the formulas could be applied to instructional materials in the armed forces and industry.

The aim of refining these readability formulas was to achieve the greatest possible predictive validity with the simplest possible means. If it could be shown that a formula with two variables (say, word-length and sentence-length) will consistently predict the reading-difficulty of a text just as accurately as more cumbersome formulas, then the simpler formula will have proved its practical validity. This in fact turned out to be the case, and despite the uneasiness of some specialists who rightly believed that the problem is much more complicated than such simple formulas suggest, one cannot just dismiss these well-tested, if narrowly conceived, empirical results.

From the high correlations achieved by these formulas, one can understand why Dr. Flesch should have been inspired to bring out a book called *The Art of Readable Writing* based on his reading ease formula:

Reading Ease = $206.835 - .846wl - 1.015sl$,
where wl = number of syllables per 100 words,
   sl = average number of words per sentence.

To which he added his Human Interest formula:

Human Interest = $3.635pw + .314ps$,
where pw = number of personal words per 100 words,
   ps = number of personal sentences per 100·sentences.

In fact, Dr. Flesch's book is a useful production which goes far beyond the expansion and defense of these formulas. It is probably as useful as many college textbooks and better informed than most.[8]

But neither Dr. Flesch's book nor any of the readability formulas touch upon some of the crucial and central issues in learning the craft of writing readable prose. Despite the usefulness of the formulas in grading textbooks for young children, they remain uninformative for the writer and the teacher of writing because they cannot discriminate between two passages which

8. R. Flesch, *The Art of Readable Writing* (New York, 1949).

score the same, yet differ substantially in readability. I take as an example a passage from Professor Bormuth that is lying open, by chance, before me.

A second question was whether or not the relationship between language variables and the difficulty of that language was linear. For example, is the difference in difficulty between two and three syllable words as great as the difficulty between seven and eight syllable words? If not, the simple correlation techniques used by early researchers yield misleading results. Bormuth (1966) found that many of the relationships showed varying degrees of curvature.[9]

My revision:

Another unanswered question about readability formulas was whether relationships such as those between reading-difficulty and word-length were constant relationships. For example, is the difference in difficulty between two and three syllable words the same as the difference in difficulty between seven and eight syllable words? If not, the simple averaging techniques of early researchers have yielded misleading results. Bormuth (1966) found that the relationships between reading difficulty and the traits used in readability formulas were in fact inconstant relationships.

When I applied existing readability formulas to these two versions, I got very similar results—just three points difference on the Flesch RE formula, and less than one grade difference on the Devereaux GP formula. Under the latter, the first version comes out as suitable for fifth graders (5.31 GP) and the second version as suitable for sixth graders (6.27 GP). Probably, these differences are statistically insignificant. What does seem to me rather telling is the mathematical pronouncement that the second version is slightly *more* difficult to read. I believe this result is false for reasons that are beyond the power of any formula to correct, since not even the complex formulas of Bormuth can factor in the semantic contrasts between semantically similar passages. It is in the nature of such formulas that *meaning*—the one thing needful —cannot be directly taken into account in assessing the readability of prose. The use of these formulas has been mainly

9. J. R. Bormuth, "New Developments in Readability Research," *Elementary English* 44 (1967): 844.

restricted to the domain of elementary education. Even there, one might hope that subjective, semantically based judgments about the readability of texts might be used to supplement the results of the formulas.

Defining Relative Readability

By introducing meaning into the concept of readability, we give up the possibility of precise arithmetical formulation. With meaning in the mix, the question we mainly want to ask is whether a piece of writing conveys its meaning without hindrance from the author's carelessness, ineptitude, or lack of craft. It is reasonable for an adult reader to gauge the readability of a text in relation to its intended meaning, not in relation to its degree of difficulty on an absolute scale. Some meanings are harder to grasp than others, and well-written texts conveying those meanings will take more time and effort to read than well-written texts conveying less arduous meanings. From this obvious truth we can infer the need for a concept of relative readability.

I will start therefore with a definition of relative readability couched in the necessary comparative terms. *Assuming that two texts convey the same meaning, the more readable text will take less time and effort to understand.* This definition, while relative to meaning, is *not* relative to individual readers, since it has now been established that a text which is more readable for a slow reader is also more readable for a fast one, and a text which is more readable for a neophyte in a subject is also more readable for an expert.[10]

The crux in this definition of relative readability is the assumption that two different texts *can* convey the same meaning. Quite reasonably, this will be a sticking point for some composition teachers, many of whom will be alert by profession to the different semantic effects of subtle differences in style. Such persons might reject the claim that in my rewriting just now of the passage from Bormuth, the overall meaning of each version is exactly the same. But I do make that claim, despite its apparent implausibility. I would go still further and say that in principle a

10. J. R. Bormuth, "Readability, a New Approach," *Reading Research Quarterly* 1 (1966): 79–132.

revision of a prose passage *must* be able to convey the same meaning as an original version, if the teaching of composition is to have any point at all.

I do not for a moment deny that my revision of the randomly chosen passage by Bormuth alters the words as well as the syntactical arrangements of the original. Yet, on my understanding of the original, the revision makes no change in the meaning of the passage as a whole. For what the passage means is not determined by adding up the meanings of individual words and sentences, as if the semantic force of a prose passage were the sum of individual units of meaning. That is not the way either speech or prose discourse normally works. In reading a prose passage longer than a few dozen words, the reader usually cannot even remember the earlier lexical and grammatical forms of the passage. By the time he reaches the end he does not remember the precise verbal forms of the beginning. It has been proved experimentally that what he mainly remembers is stored as meaning, not as language; and it is meaning, not linguistic form, which provides him with a context for understanding the part of the discourse he is currently reading.[11] This is the normal pattern (though not the universal pattern) in understanding speech.

A short lyric poem does not, of course, conform to this normal pattern of linguistic forgetfulness. Yet most forms of writing, particularly the commoner forms of prose, are not read with the slowness and attention to form appropriate to the reading of lyric poetry. And even poetry is less exacting in its mnemonic demands than is sometimes assumed. Almost everyone who quotes poetry without checking the text misquotes it. The poet himself, like the humblest writer of prose, realizes that his semantic intentions are conveyed equally well (or badly) by alternative verbal forms, and he sometimes fails to decide which version will convey his

11. This important finding, reconfirmed by several researchers, is described in the following publications: S. Fillenbaum, "Memory for Gist: Some Relevant Variables," *Language and Speech* 9 (1966): 217–27; J. S. Sachs, "Recognition Memory for Syntactic and Semantic Aspects of Connected Discourse," *Perception and Psychophysics* 2 (1967): 437–42; P. N. Johnson-Laird, "The Perception and Memory of Sentences," in *New Horizons in Linguistics*, ed. J. Lyons (Harmondsworth, 1970), pp. 261–70; W. J. M. Levelt and G. Kempen, "Semantic and Syntactic Aspects of Remembering Sentences: A Review of Some Recent Continental Research," in *Studies in Long Term Memory*, ed. A. Kennedy and A. Wilkes (London, 1975), pp. 201–18. W. F. Brewer, "Memory for Ideas: Synonym Substitution," *Memory and Cognition* 3 (1975): 458–64.

intentions best. This stylistic flexibility of poetry has been documented in detail by Professor E. A. J. Honigmann in his valuable
book on the problems of establishing a poetic text.[12] His central
example is Shakespeare, who, as a writer for the theater, would
have recognized the semantic irrelevance of certain variations in
stage language which, once spoken, is heard no more.

In another book, I have taken into account all of the objections
against the possibility that two different texts can carry exactly
the same meaning.[13] I shall not repeat those detailed arguments
here. My intention here has been to say just enough to make the
concept of relative readability a plausible and useful concept.
For, unless it were possible for a revised text to convey the same
meaning as the original in a more readable way, we would not
need to teach a student how to write readable prose. The student
who protests that he *did* say what he meant would be right, and
the teacher of composition could close up shop.

What the ideal teacher of composition does teach is a skill that
enables his students to convey their meanings efficiently. Per-
suasiveness, clarity, elegance may be parts of the student's
semantic intentions, or they may not be. Such qualities are not
universal qualities of readable prose, because they are not
universal semantic intentions for all writers at all times. The
composition teacher is not by profession a tyrant who tells his
students what they ought to *mean*, though he may consider such
instruction a secondary pedagogical duty.

Let me give a brief example of the disconnection between
clarity of thought and readability of prose. The following short
passage begins a chapter of *An Introduction to Logic* by Cohen
and Nagel, an excellent and generally well-written book.

> In the previous chapters we have seen that the validity of a
> demonstration depends not on the truth or falsity of the prem-
> ises, but upon their form or structure. We have therefore been
> compelled to recognize that the fundamental task of logic is the
> study of these objective relations between propositions which
> condition the inferences by which we pass from premises to
> conclusions.[14]

12. E. A. J. Honigman, *The Stability of Shakespeare's Text* (Lincoln, Neb-
raska, 1965).
13. *The Aims of Interpretation* (Chicago, 1976), pp. 50–73.
14. M. Cohen and E. Nagel, *An Introduction to Logic and Scientific Method*
(New York, 1934).

The clarity of *thought* in that passage could scarcely be improved upon; and it would be presumptuous of me to "correct" the thinking of two first-class logicians. But the relative readability of the excerpt can be rather easily improved. As the passage stands, it takes more time and effort to understand than its meaning requires. Here is a revision:

> In previous chapters we saw that valid logic depends on the form of a demonstration rather than on the truth of its premises. That compelled us to view the main task of logic as a study of the purely formal relations between propositions. For only these purely formal relations can determine the logical validity of our inferences from premises to conclusions.

The contrary sort of example—where the writing is highly readable and clear, but the thought is muddy—is often to be found in the letter columns of British newspapers. Here is an example from *TLS:*

> In advancing an ideologically neutral approach to women's history, Dr. Harrison does a grave injustice to the work of the new feminist polemicists. . . . The adoption of a non-ideological approach is especially harmful to those working in the Victorian period. The "position of women" question in the last century was as highly charged an issue as it is today. The fact that many ordinary women were anti-feminist does not mean they were living in an ideologically neutral universe. [15]

This passage is easily read and understood. But while the writing is clear, the thought is not, for the passage states in effect the following illogical argument:

> Because the *situation* to be described by the historian is not ideologically neutral, his *account* of that situation should not be ideologically neutral.

This is a straightforward non sequitur, built on a semantic slippage from an "ideologically neutral approach" to an "ideologically neutral universe." But the very repetitions of these phrases help make the prose readable and clearly understood.

These examples suggest that the relative readability of prose, and even its relative "clarity," are governed more by psychological principles than by logical ones. The logic of writing is not the same as the logic of thought, and the clarity of a piece of

15. December 19, 1975, p. 1517.

writing is not the same as the clarity of its thought. Even if conceptual clarity could be taught in a composition course, such instruction might divert attention from the psychological principles that chiefly govern the readability of writing.

Before turning to those principles, I shall offer a last, brief reminder of the difference between relative readability and the concept of reading ease. Reading ease, by itself, is a narrow criterion which fails as a universal normative principle for writing. It is an oversimplification, even a trivialization of the norm that I have advocated here. To reduce the danger that a reader might entertain such a misunderstanding, I shall, in what follows, occasionally substitute the phrase "intrinsic effectiveness" for "relative readability." The substitution is less descriptive than the original, and I shall use it sparingly, but it will serve as a reminder that relative readability is an intrinsic and truly universal norm of writing.

5 The Psychological Bases of Readability

The Psychological Bases of Readability

Identifying the Problem

A good writer knows how to compose and revise effectively without necessarily knowing the principles behind his proficiency. E. B. White said that he learned to write prose as he learned to drive a car—without understanding what went on under the hood. In that respect, William Tilden, the great tennis player, was a more philosophical student of his craft than E. B. White. Tilden acknowledged that you can play good tennis without knowing why and without following any textbook technique. He observed that excellent players broke the rules by performing diverse yet equally effective movements in executing their strokes—wrong-footing the ball, hitting it on the run, and so on. Considering this diversity of successful tennis techniques, Tilden deduced a principle that must rank as a truly philosophical principle of the tennis stroke: the only thing that matters is the movement of the racket face during the split second when it stays in contact with the ball. How the successful motion is achieved is secondary. All the multifarious maxims of tennis, some of which contradict each other, can be ignored if the stroke is effective.

The application of Tilden's principle to the rules and maxims of composition is obvious. What counts is the effective conveyance of one's meaning during the time when somebody is reading one's text. And just as the laws of physics govern the flight of a tennis ball that has been hit in a certain way by a moving racket, so the psychological principles of language reception govern the effectiveness of actual prose. The maxims of composition are, of course, related to these psychological principles, just as tennis maxims like weight-shift and follow-through are related to the laws of physics. And similarly, the great diversity and contradictions of writing maxims can be resolved only by referring them to root psychological principles which determine their relations and their importance. These relationships between root principles and practical maxims will be a subject of my next chapter. In this chapter, I shall try to isolate the psychological principles themselves.

This will be an exceedingly difficult task. The psychology of language reception is still very imperfectly understood, and the bulk of experimentation in the subject has been limited to words and sentences in isolation. Work on language reception in actual speech transactions and in the reading of actual texts has been rather rare, despite general agreement that actual language processing is different in several respects from the processing of isolated words and sentences in test situations. But experiments with longer stretches of discourse present the experimenter with grave problems of interpretation and control. Consequently, despite the great quantity of interesting work in the field, my own inferences from the psychological literature must be at times tentative and conjectural.

A second difficulty is to isolate the principles governing readability from the principles governing language reception in general. The large-scale reception models are the subject of much dispute in any case, and to present them in detail would distract attention from the problem at hand, since any general model of language processing will govern alike prose that is readable and prose that is not. A more narrow focus on the factors that affect the ease or difficulty of prose will make possible the deduction of some important conclusions without a premature commitment to any single psychological model of language reception.

Similarly, by focusing on the reception of longer stretches of discourse, I may be able to avoid premature inferences from atomistic experimentation. For instance, research on isolated sentences has shown that actives are processed more easily than passives, and affirmatives more easily than negatives.[1] On the

1. D. R. Olson and N. Filby, "On the Comprehension of Active and Passive Sentences," *Cognitive Psychology* 3 (1972): 361–81; M. A. Just and P. A. Carpenter, "Comprehension of Negation with Quantification," *Journal of Verbal Learning and Verbal Behavior* 10 (1971): 244–53.

other hand, my own subjective experiments have persuaded me that these results can be reversed in connected discourse, if one places an active sentence amidst a series of passives or an affirmative amidst a series of negative sentences. This tentative result will surprise no teacher of composition and has, as I shall argue, significant implications for the psychology of readability.

I should make one further introductory observation. Some of the most important data concerning the psychology of language processing has come from studies of oral speech. For reasons which I shall mention later, many of these results are directly applicable to writing. I have already acknowledged in Chapter 1 the impossibility of drawing an absolute, functional boundary between oral and written speech. To this concession may be added strong empirical evidence that *listenability* and *readability* are the same. Fang has demonstrated a .96 correlation between his listenability test and the Flesch Reading Ease formula, while Sticht's experiments have shown "no differences between reading and listening scores" within carefully graded test groups. [2] These findings have important implications for the psychology and also the pedagogy of readability.

Why the "Cloze" Method Indicates Readability

In the 1950s, Wilson L. Taylor, a doctoral student in psychology, developed a system for measuring readability that was quite unlike any of the standard formulas. [3] Instead of measuring word familiarity and sentence length, his method measured the percentage of correct guesses which a test group made when blank spaces were inserted in a prose sample to replace every fifth or sixth word. The relative ability of the test group to make correct guesses in different prose samples showed a high correlation with the readability scores of those samples as computed under the standard readability formulas. Why should that be so?

Taylor's experiments had two sources of inspiration: information theory and Gestalt psychology. From information theory he

2. I. E. Fang, "The Easy Listening Formula," *Journal of Broadcasting* 11 (1966–67): 63–68; T. G. Sticht, "Learning by Listening," in *Language Comprehension and the Acquisition of Knowledge*, ed. J. B. Carroll and R. D. Freedle (Washington, D.C., 1972), p. 288.

3. W. L. Taylor, "Application of Cloze and Entropy Measures to the Study of Contextual Constraint in Samples of Continuous Prose," doctoral thesis, University of Illinois, 1954, *Dissertation Abstracts* 15 (1955): 464–65.

took the idea of measuring the amount of "redundancy" in a message by determining how much of it could be deleted without changing its conveyed meaning. From Gestalt psychology he took the concept of pattern completion, whereby certain familiar or "good" patterns (usually visual) could be completed by a test-subject even though some elements of the pattern had been deleted. Gestalt psychologists called such completion "closure," because the result was an organized form which seemed subjectively perfected or closed. From this use of "closure," Taylor devised the jargon phrase "cloze procedure" to describe his method.

Subsequently, it was discovered that the cloze method yielded results which correlated not only with readability scores but also with reading-comprehension scores. [4] The cloze score seemed to predict more accurately than readability formulas just how much a reader would understand and remember from a prose passage. As Taylor observed, readability formulas by themselves will equate Gertrude Stein's prose with the prose of an elementary-school text, although the relative comprehensibility of the texts will differ enormously. On the other hand, proponents of the formulas reply that the cloze method is rather impractical, since the whole point of readability formulas is to predict the readability of a text before children are subjected to it. No doubt the cloze method is rather impractical as a substitute for readability formulas, but it has proved itself to be a more sensitive indicator of readability than the formulas. I have chosen to discuss the cloze method here because its peculiar efficacy can be explained only by introducing some of the psychological principles that I shall be discussing later in this chapter. Some conjectures about why the method works will serve as a general introduction to my separate discussions of different topics.

The most paradoxical result of the cloze experiments is that readers often learn most from a text which gives them the least "information" in the technical sense of that word. Information, according to information theory, is the reduction of uncertainty, and if a word in a text is so highly predictable that it will be guessed even if deleted, then that word carries very little information. Under this conception of information, very little is added if the correct completion of *Once upon a* ———— is the

4. W. L. Taylor, Cloze Readability Scores as Indices of Individual Differences in Comprehension and Aptitude," *Journal of Applied Psychology* 41 (1957): 19–26.

word *time*, whereas a great deal of information is added if the text word is *mattress*. On the other hand, since a word carrying more information is less likely to be predicted, sentences with such words would yield a very low cloze score. And since a low cloze score indicates that relatively little will be effectively learned from the text, it follows that one tends to assimilate less information in the ordinary sense from a text that is very rich in information in the technical sense. In fact, the ultimately informative text, in the technical sense, would be nonsense, because the predictability of any deleted word would approach zero.

A closely related paradox, particularly for written language, is that the longer way can be the shorter way. In oral speech, where elliptical phrasing is the norm, one can successfully convey meaning by language so rich in "information" that it might yield a zero cloze score when transcribed to paper. Apparently, therefore, readability and comprehensibility are enhanced if the text makes rather small, predictable leaps from one word to the next, sometimes using five or six words, if necessary, instead of two or three. Here is a sentence from G. A. Miller, an excellent stylist, whose work happens to be on my desk:

> In English we recognize immediately that an error has occurred if we read in our newspaper, "Man bites dxg." [5]

We can shorten this sentence without changing its sense by merely omitting the relative:

> In English we recognize immediately an error has occurred if we read in our newspaper, "Man bites dxg."

But this sentence is *less* readable and will take longer to process than its longer version. Omitting the *that* has reduced its local predictabilities, causing it to get a lower cloze-score. That is immediately apparent if we blank out some of the words:

> In English we recognize ——— an error ——— occurred if we read in our ———, "Man bites dxg."

or

> In English we recognize ——— that an error ——— occurred if we read in our ———, "Man bites dxg."

5. G. A. Miller and J. A. Selfridge, "Verbal Context and the Recall of Meaningful Material," *American Journal of Psychology* 63 (1950): 177.

This example can serve only as a provisional illustration, since the cloze method works properly only within a longer stretch of discourse. That is one reason it is the most accurate method now available for measuring readability. A cloze test takes into account the wider verbal context within which the blank space occurs, and therefore factors in both semantic and syntactic expectations. Hence, the proper way to administer the cloze test is to present a fairly long stretch of unmutilated text before beginning to blank out individual words.

It is obvious that the cloze test directly measures the average predictability of text words for a particular group of readers. Far less obvious is the reason for a direct correlation between word predictability and readability. To explain this correlation, we will have to discover those aspects of word predictability which make a text easier to process and understand. To isolate these aspects, it may be useful to apply another cloze test to two passages which convey the same meaning but differ in actual readability. For the sake of brevity, I will compare the short passage from Bormuth with my revision of it, deleting in each case every fifth word. The reader is invited to make his own subjective experiment with the two mutilated passages.

Bormuth:

A second question was ———— or not the relationship ————
language variables and the ———— of that language was
————. For example, is the ———— in difficulty between two
———— three syllable words as ———— as the difficulty between
———— and eight syllable words? ———— not, the simple correlation ———— used by early researchers ———— misleading
results. Bormuth ———— that many of the ———— showed varying degrees of ————.

My revision:

A second unanswered question ———— readability formulas
was whether ———— such as those between ———— difficulty
and word length ———— constant relationships. For example,
———— the difference in difficulty ———— two and three syllable ———— the same as the ———— in difficulty between seven
———— eight syllable words? If ————, the simple averaging
techniques ———— early researchers have yielded ———— results. Bormuth found that ———— relationships between reading difficulty ———— and the traits used ———— readability
formulas were in ———— inconstant relationships.

The revised version will score higher for most readers, with or without contextualization, mainly because its local probabilities are higher. Because it is more explicit, repetitious, and jargon-free than the original, its words will be easier to predict.

The connection between the predictability of contextualized prose and its easiness to read seems to lie in the relationship between word predictability and speed of processing. If the word you encounter is a word you expected to encounter, then you will process that word faster. For ease of processing is equivalent to speed of processing. The sequential maneuvers of speech reception are going forward at an average *maximum* rate of something like 200 milliseconds per word.[6] Since this approximate rate cannot be exceeded, there is a direct relation between the rate of reception and the amount of effort that goes into processing a given length of discourse.

But why does word predictability speed up the rate of processing? A number of slightly different answers have been proposed, all of which converge on some kind of matching or decision-making activity which is being performed on the incoming words.[7] The words have to be matched with the preceding discourse, and they have to be matched with syntactic-semantic categories. If the first attempt at matching results in a good fit, then we go forward to process more words. But if the fit is bad,

6. A number of results converge on this maximal figure of 200 milliseconds per word. 1. The maximum reading rate for adults is about 300 words per minute, where the words average two syllables. The claims made for faster rates in speed reading are illusory (see E. J. Gibson and H. Levin, *The Psychology of Reading*, [Cambridge, Mass., 1975], pp. 539–49). 2. Sperling has shown that the maximal processing rate for highly familiar syllable sequences is about ten syllables per second—again 200 milliseconds per two-syllable word (G. Sperling, "A Model for Visual Memory Tasks," in *Information-Processing Approaches to Visual Perception*, ed. R. N. Haber [New York, 1969], p. 28). 3. An absolute limitation of the mind's speed of operation is 50 milliseconds per minimal item (see A. B. Kristofferson, "Attention and Psychophysical Time," *Acta Psychologica* 27 [1967]: 93–100.) Allowing for slight variations among individuals, this figure is regarded by psychobiologists as firmly established. The relation between the minimum of 100 milliseconds per syllable and a minimum of 50 milliseconds per item of perception will be discussed later in the chapter.

7. On matching procedures in language processing, see: D. E. Broadbent, "Word Frequency Effect and Response Bias," *Psychological Review* 74 (1967): 1–15; D. B. Fry, "Speech Reception and Perception," in J. Lyons, ed. *New Horizons in Linguistics* (Harmondsworth, England, 1970), pp. 29–52; T. Trabasso, "Mental Operations in Language Comprehension," in Carroll and Freedle, *Language and the Acquisition of Knowledge*, pp. 113–37.

we need to posit still further syntactic-semantic categories until we do achieve a good fit. In some cases, we may even need to revise our previous constructions of the passage in order to achieve a successful decision. Obviously, a success in the first matching attempt will result in a faster rate of processing than will a further continuation of the decision-making procedure. Hence, an increase in word predictability will increase the number of successful first attempts and will speed up the process of understanding.

What the cloze method directly tests is the average *local* predictability of words in their actual context. This local predictability is therefore far more relevant to actual speed of processing than is the *general* predictability of a word as determined by its position on the Thorndike-Lorge word-frequency list. That is one reason why cloze measurements are in principle more accurate and informative than any readability formula could be.

Where the cloze method might seem to suffer is in its failure to consider, as do some of the formulas, the effects of syntactical complexity. The taker of a cloze test is given plenty of time to complete his guesses, though a reader may be slowed down by hard syntax, even when he ultimately finds the words of the text highly predictable. On the other hand, this apparent theoretical defect is overcome by the undoubted correlation between ease of syntax and word predictability. Speed of syntactical processing depends upon word predictability just as much as does speed of lexical processing. The expectation that a word will belong to a certain grammatical category and will perform a certain kind of grammatical function is just as much an element in its local predictability as its expected semantic force.

Even abnormal syntax and abnormal vocabulary can become the norm for a text that is long enough. That is why cloze measurements, properly administered, can be highly sensitive gauges for the readability of widely different texts for widely different groups of readers. And that is why the cloze test does indicate the processing time that a text will require (and hence its absolute readability) for a given category of readers.

Uncertainty and Constraint in
Language Processing

Probably one reason that information theory has proved to be a powerful tool of psychological research is that its concepts approximate certain actual functions of the mind, particularly certain functions of language processing. Although the methods of information theory have tended to be highly mathematical, some of its central concepts are mainly psychological; among these, two crucial ones are *uncertainty* and *uncertainty reduction*. Of course, not just information theory but also probability theory is concerned with the measurement of uncertainty. (Probability theory has been well-named "the logic of uncertainty.") The more specific contribution of information theory has been in describing linguistic communication as an ongoing process of uncertainty reduction. This does, in fact, seem to be an important feature of our actual reception of language. As I suggested in discussing the cloze method, the efficiency of language reception depends on decreasing the amount and duration of the reader's uncertainty wherever possible in a text.

One of the more familiar terms for linguistic uncertainty is *ambiguity*, a word which can imply both grammatical and semantic uncertainty. Among grammatical theorists, the current example of ambiguity is the following sentence:

Flying airplanes can be dangerous,

where the example is understood to be gramatically uncertain or ambiguous, even though the surface grammar is stable. The sentence can mean:

It can be dangerous to fly airplanes.

or

It can be dangerous to be (on the
ground) near flying airplanes

But the uncertainty of the sentence is far greater than this suggests. Indeed, the semantic uncertainty of any sentence in isolation tends to be indefinitely great, though we usually ignore its uncertainty by giving it some definite meaning. For instance, the sentence could be used to mean:

It can be dangerous to pilot airplanes.
It can be an expensive addiction to pilot
airplanes.
It can be dangerous to fly in airplanes.
It can be dangerous to guide model airplanes by radio control.
etc.

Any sentence in isolation is semantically uncertain, because it can mean whatever it might mean in an indefinite number of actual uses. That is one reason for the unreliability of some linguistic experiments with isolated words and sentences. Their perceived uncertainty varies from person to person, and their inherent semantic uncertainty is almost limitless.

In these remarks, I have been using *uncertainty* in the ordinary, unquantified sense, rather than in the numerical sense imposed by information theory. While the ordinary usage is preferable here, I shall nonetheless borrow some quantitative results from the information theorists. The important results for our purposes are those which show a rather precise relation between the amount of uncertainty in a language stimulus and the amount of time required to recognize or interpret the stimulus.[8] This general fact has been known among experimental psychologists since the second half of the nineteenth century. It was first given precision by W. E. Hick, who demonstrated in 1952 that reaction time increased linearly as the logarithm of the number of possible stimuli, when each stimulus has an equal probability of occurrence.[9] This result has since been confirmed by a number of later experiments.[10]

This average result means that the longer time required to interpret an uncertain signal results from a series of successive matching attempts. Apparently, the actual signal is successively matched against the different plausible signals that could occur in that particular situation. This processing model gets confirmation from further studies which show that reaction time will decrease for some signals when the experimenter increases the expectancy or predictability of those particular signals.[11] Broadbent, in a classic article, proposed an explanation of this "response bias" by suggesting a correlation between reaction time and the subject's sense of a signal's probability.[12] All of these results lend support to my speculation that a cloze test will indicate the readability of prose by indicating its average subjective uncertainty, and hence the average speed with which it can be processed.

8. See W. R. Garner, *Uncertainty and Structure as Psychological Concepts*, (New York, 1962), p. 39.

9. W. E. Hick, "On the Rate of Gain of Information," *Quarterly Journal of Experimental Psychology* 4 (1952): 11–26.

10. Garner, *Uncertainty and Structure*, pp. 40–41.

11. E. R. F. W. Crossman, "Entropy and Choice Time," *Quarterly Journal of Experimental Psychology* 5 (1953): 41–51.

12. D. E. Broadbent, "Word Frequency Effect and Response Bias," pp. 1–15.

If uncertainty lengthens the time required to process language, any technique which reduces uncertainty will shorten language processing. And the only way to reduce uncertainty is to reduce the number of plausible alternatives which must pass through our matching-monitor before a stretch of discourse is understood. That is to say, we must reduce uncertainty by reducing the number of semantic-syntactic candidates at any point in the discourse. Now, we reduce the number of these potential candidates by *increasing* the subjective probability of a few of them. In the parlance of information theory, we reduce uncertainty by increasing *constraint*. In prose discourse, earlier signals exercise constraint upon succeeding ones by reducing the number of plausible candidates. In readable prose, these will be reduced to a very few, each having a high subjective probability. With this large amount of constraint, the time and effort required for processing will be small.

Constraint is a precise, functional term for *context*. Everyone knows that we understand language with reference to its context, yet that vague formulation suggests nothing about the actual function of context in language processing. Its actual function is to impose constraints on the syntactic and semantic possibilities of speech. Because of the sequential character of language, these contextual constraints ought to be greater in the middle of a discourse than at the beginning, and this has been confirmed for words as well as for sentences by G. A. Miller and his associates.[13] A directly practical implication of this psychological fact is that the beginning of a sentence, and particularly of a whole discourse, should be made very constraining. Beginnings also have the greatest psychological impact; they are more closely attended to and more firmly remembered than middles and ends. It follows that the readability of prose will be greatly enhanced by increasing the constraining power of beginnings.

The constraint of beginnings has, in addition, a psychological force greater than the average local predictabilities of the ongoing discourse. This is an important phenomenon which I shall call "short-term expectancy." Suppose we know in advance that the discourse as a whole will consist of many monosyllabic words

13. G. A. Miller, G. A. Heise, and W. Lichter, "The Intelligibility of Speech as a Function of the Context of the Test Materials," *Journal of Experimental Psychology* 41 (1951): 329–35; G. A. Miller and S. Isard, "Some Perceptual Consequences of Linguistic Rules," *Journal of Verbal Learning and Verbal Behavior* 2 (1963): 217–28.

but only a few disyllabic words, in an average ratio of 80% to 20%. Knowing this, we are then given several test sentences of the following sort:

The man in the car drove backwards and then he called
the ——— (*cops, police*). Choose 1.

There will be a tendency in favor of *cops* in this example. But if the test sentence is:

The man in the car drove backwards and then he summoned
the ——— (*law, police*). Choose 1.

For reasons I will give shortly, there will be a tendency in favor of *police*, despite the fact that our long-term expectancy predicts a monosyllable.

Hake has shown that when subjects are asked to guess which of two events will occur, and they know in advance that the occurrences will be 20% versus 80%, they will guess the unlikely event 20% of the time and the likely event only 80% of the time.[14] Yet their *optimal* scores would be achieved if they simply guessed the more probable event 100% of the time. Why do we act against our long-term expectancy in this way? I believe that our tendency to do so is highly useful in coping with reality and hence might have a basis in biological evolution. We act against our long-term expectancy in a specific context because we tend to assume that the pattern of the new situation will continue in a uniform way, even though that pattern is unlike the general long-term pattern of the past. We seem to posit a subclass of events, different from the larger class, on the basis of very few, very recent clues. This is practically useful to us, because the short-term probabilities of a local experience are usually more reliable than general long-term probabilities. In effect, we narrow the present event-class, and assume the uniformity of that narrow class. This is exactly parallel to self-conscious, scientific judgments of probability, where the reliability of results is increased when the class of events is narrowed.

One aspect of this short-term expectancy has an important but neglected application to the readability of prose. I refer to the rhythmical patterns of prose discourse. In one of his aperçus, Herbert Spencer suggested that poetry is often easier to read than

14. H. W. Hake, "The Perception of Frequency of Occurrence, and the Development of Expectancy in Human Experimental Subjects," in *Information Theory in Psychology*, ed. H. Quastler (Glencoe, Ill., 1955).

prose because of the greater predictability of its rhythm. If that is correct, as I believe it is, then the handbooks on composition have paid too little attention to prose rhythm. In the test sentences just quoted, it is obvious that the chosen pattern-continuations were also rhythmical continuations:

then he called the cops

vs.

then he summoned the police.

Some studies have indicated that actual speech patterns tend to be isochronous, suggesting that we tend to continue rhythmical patterns in the production as well as in the reception of speech.[15] Such short-term expectancies, based on pattern continuations, could be termed "small-scale constraints." They are the expectancies induced by the local verbal context.

But, obviously, the larger-scale context of prose is still more important than small-scale constraints in reducing uncertainty and enhancing readability. In an earlier chapter I observed that one of the distinctive traits of written as opposed to oral speech was the lack in writing of a situational context to constrain meaning possibilities. From this I inferred that written language had to introduce these constraints explicitly into the text itself. On the other hand, if *all* contextual constraints were made explicit, prose would drift towards the unreadability of highly explicit legal documents. Even in prose, therefore, the greater amount of contextual constraint remains invisible, like the base of an iceberg.

This invisible context is enormously constraining. It consists of linguistic "rules" and semantic conventions. It embraces large domains of tacitly shared knowledge, and it includes tacit suppositions about the theme and tendency of the text as a whole. The character of these "covert semantic assumptions and presuppositions" has been well-described by Carroll and Freedle, who call for more research into this subject.[16] Certainly, one empirical confirmation of this covert, contextual constraint is the large variation in cloze-test scores among different classes of readers. This suggests that readability does largely depend on the writer's

15. See W. Thomson, *The Rhythm of Speech* (Glascow, 1923). I am grateful to J. C. Pope for this reference.

16. Carroll and Freedle, *Language Comprehension and the Acquisition of Knowledge*, p. 360.

correct assessment of the relevant knowledge already possessed by his principal audience. This tacit knowledge is perhaps the chief component of large-scale contextual constraint. A shrewd decision about the knowledge that the writer can tacitly assume in his audience may be the most important decision the writer makes.

Nonetheless, a neglect of these large-scale covert constraints is rarely the chief cause of unreadable writing. Most users of language know that we need to explain more to strangers than we do to intimates. Practical experience tells us that the main uncertainties of bad writing are small-scale, local uncertainties, persisting from word to word and sentence to sentence. These are the uncertainties that slow down and confuse the reader, and to these transient uncertainties I shall devote much of the rest of this chapter.

The Exigencies of Attention

The time it takes to process a given stretch of discourse is largely determined by its local uncertainties, because, as we have seen, more uncertainties will require more successive matching-operations before the reader experiences a click of understanding. If several of these matching operations in the mind could take place simultaneously, a modest increase in local uncertainty might not slow down our reading. But experiments since the nineteenth century have consistently shown a linear relation between the amount of our uncertainty and the amount of time we require to interpret a stimulus. It appears, therefore, that we are unable to carry out several matching operations simultaneously and that we must process them successively, one at a time. It is now known that the maximum rate for conducting these successive matchings is about twenty items per second.[17]

This absolute limit on our speed of processing constitutes, therefore, a mental bottleneck which cannot be circumvented. What is the character of this bottleneck? We know that one of its functions is to match a linguistic stimulus with a succession of semantic-syntactic candidates until we achieve a good fit. If the kind of stimulus we actually receive is the kind we expected, then we will need to generate only a few candidates before achieving a fit. This matching, or decision-making, function is the active

17. See note 6 to this chapter.

center as well as the temporal bottleneck of linguistic understanding. Moreover, if this central monitor turns aside to perform
its function on some nonlinguistic stimulus, then linguistic processing comes to a halt. If, for instance, my mind wanders while I
am reading a book, I can come to the end of a page before
realizing that I have not really understood what my eyes have
taken in. I was not "paying attention." I will then have to go back
to the place where mind started to wander, and reread the whole
passage. The same thing happens in oral discourse. One says,
"Excuse me, would you please say that again, I wasn't paying
attention."

Thus, our linguistic bottleneck is obviously connected in some
way with the phenomenon of attention. The feature of one-thing-
at-a-time in our linguistic monitor is the distinctive feature of
attention. Although the individual objects of attention can be rich
and complex, they must nonetheless be unified objects, for we
cannot pay attention simultaneously to several discrete objects.
Whenever we appear to do so, we are undoubtedly shifting
attention back and forth very rapidly, as we do when we follow
two different themes in polyphonic music.[18] A good way of
describing the relation between linguistic uncertainty and speed of
processing is to say that high expectancy lures our attention to the
right address much sooner than low expectancy does. Attention
has to go to fewer addresses per unit of discourse, and therefore
gets less tired out.

The phenomenon of attention is so familiar that it needn't be
discussed here at length. The danger is that its very familiarity
might lead us to neglect its fundamental importance to readability. It is obvious that every shift of attention takes time, so that
every unsuccessful shift of attention induced by local uncertainties
will cost wasted time and effort in the reading process. It is also
obvious that prose which fails to hold and control our attention
will be arduous and unreadable prose. Readability therefore
depends on several exigencies of attention. Readable prose must, as
we have seen, require few shifts of attention between individual

18. For discussions of attention shifting, see: D. E. Broadbent, *Perception and
Communication* (Oxford, 1958), pp. 210–43; A. T. Welford, "Evidence of a
Single Channel Decision Mechanism Limiting Performance in a Serial Reaction
Task," *Quarterly Journal of Experimental Psychology* 11 (1959): 193–210; M. C.
Smith, "Theories of the Psychological Refraction Period," *Psychological Bulletin*,
67 (1967): 202–13.

words. It must also require very few shifts of attention between sentences. And it must steadily hold the reader's attention over still longer stretches of discourse comprising many sentences.

These large-scale exigencies of attention are not strictly the same as the writer's duty to be interesting. The wandering of an uninterested reader's mind is sometimes beyond the control of even the best writer, and the woolgathering-quotient of prose will vary greatly with different readers at different times. The composition handbooks inform us that an arresting image or metaphor will tend to hold a reader's attention. But such flagwaving could in some cases distract attention from the main semantic goals of a discourse. A more truly universal principle of attention-holding is that of thematic focus. To avoid wasteful attention shifts, the verbal theme of one phrase must be similar to the theme of the preceding phrase. The expectancies set up by one phrase should be fulfilled in the next. That is to say, the reader's attention should have to go to only a few nearby addresses before finding the right one.[19] This principle of attention constraint is a universal principle of readability, and it operates on the large scale as well as the small.

But paradoxically, a constantly narrow constraint on attention can by itself induce shifts of attention. Prose that constantly fulfills expectations exactly as the reader thinks that it will, will be boring prose. Very continuous and very high predictability is the essence of boredom. Attention gets tired of going to the same address, just as it gets tired of going to a lot of wrong addresses. This paradoxical phenomenon has been confirmed experimentally: when all possible effects of fatigue are excluded from the computation, monotony, by itself, will cause a deterioration of attention in all kinds of circumstances.[20] This fact substantiates Herbert Spencer's suggestion of 1852 that variety in style actually lessens reader effort. It appears, therefore, that readability requires both a narrow constraint on attention and also a looseness of constraint. In good prose, this conflict is resolved by making intelligent compromises between the two opposing factors. This is one of several fundamental conflicts in the psychology of readability, and these conflicts are a topic to which I shall return in the final section of this chapter.

19. The practical implications of this principle are drawn in the section on "Advancing Composition Research" of this chapter.
20. Broadbent, *Perception and Communication*, pp. 135–38.

Clause, Closure and
Short-Term Memory

It is an old idea that the clause (or clause-sentence) is the primary unit of speech. Cassirer, discussing all known language types in his *Philosophy of Symbolic Forms* in 1953, traced the insight back to von Humboldt. Recently, the primacy of the clause has received imposing support from ingenious experiments which have shown that clauses in English are more directly perceived than their constituent individual words! [21] Moreover, it has been shown that, in compound sentences, clause length rather than overall sentence length is the relevant factor in readability scores. Since no one doubts that we take in the words of a clause one after another before we perceive and understand the clause itself, we need an explanation of the paradoxical finding that "the clause is the primary perceptual unit." [22]

The most probable explanation of the paradox is that we suspend some of our final decisions about the syntactic-semantic functions of the constituent words until after we have decided on the meaning of the clause. We perceive the constituent words and phrases in a definite way only after we have achieved semantic closure. *Clause* is therefore related to *closure* by psychological function as well as by etymology.

No doubt this explanation is oversimple. Very probably, some phrase-units and individual words are assigned rather definite functions before the clause is complete. But the basic insight that the whole is prior to the parts in language perception must be roughly accurate. It is an observation that seems to hold even for our perception of words. Some ingenious research has shown that words are more directly perceived than their constituent phonemes. [23] If these experimental findings are correct, and I suspect that they are, it follows that language processing must entail some kind of reviewing procedure whereby everything must pass by the attention-monitor twice: perceived the first time as a

21. T. G. Bever, "The Influence of Speech Performance on Linguistic Structures," in *Advances in Psycholinguistics*, ed. G. B. Flores d'Arcais and W. J. M. Levelt (Amsterdam, 1970).

22. Quoted from T. G. Bever, "Perception, Thought and Language," in Carroll and Freedle, *Language Comprehension and the Acquisition of Knowledge*.

23. H. Savin and T. G. Bever, "The Non-perceptual Reality of the Phoneme," *Journal of Verbal Learning and Verbal Behavior* 3 (1970): 295–302.

sequence of not yet fully determined linguistic functions and perceived the second time more holistically and definitely as a semantic unit. Intuitively, one feels that this scanning-plus-review model is too simple. But even if the review process often occurs at the phrase level, with semantic closure being partly achieved before the clause is completed, the process would still be a review process whereby the provisional interpretations of phrases are being continually confirmed or altered in a definite way as the words unfold.

This deduction about a twice-performed sequence in language processing correlates well with experimental data concerning the maximum rates for reading or hearing easy English prose. The maximum accurate reading rate is about 300 words per minute— or about ten syllables per second. This is just one-half our maximum processing rate of twenty times per second, suggesting that the maximum reading rate even of the easiest prose involves a scanning-plus-reviewing procedure through our attention-monitor. This arithmetical correlation is striking even if some polysyllabic words are read as simple ideographs. My contention that ideographic reading cannot be an important factor is confirmed by experiments with accelerated *oral* speech. Even after practice with rapid listening-rates, people cannot accurately understand rapid discourse above a definite rate. This maximum rate is 300 words per minute—again ten syllables per second.[24] After that point there is a sharp drop in comprehension that cannot be elevated by training. Every clause that is read once is probably read twice.

The clause, then, is the primary perceptual unit of all languages because it is the minimal unit that has semantic determinacy. The constituent words of a clause become perceptually determinate only when they are perceived as functional elements within the clause, and these definite functions are fully determined only after the whole clause is perceived. This genuine linguistic universal is based upon a universal of the human mind. The mind sets a limit on the duration of any temporal sequence that can be perceived as a unit. Since speech is produced and received as a temporal sequence of elements, all languages require the use of a bracketing mechanism—the clause—which

24. D. B. Orr, H. L. Friedman, and J. C. Williams, "Trainability of Listening Comprehension of Speeded Discourse," *Journal of Educational Psychology* 56 (1965): 148–56.

consolidates a sequence of elements into a definitely perceived semantic unit. We can speak only in clauses, and we can receive speech only in clauses. If we examine more closely the mechanism behind this universal linguistic necessity, we will be able to infer some of the factors which affect the readability of clauses.

The first function to consider is the attention-monitor. Its limitation to one frame at a time, and to twenty frames per second must be reckoned with, not only for language reception but for perceptual experience in general. If this attention-monitor were the only mechanism of perception, it would be hard to conceive how we could ever perceive complex wholes. At any moment we would be perceiving only what was passing by the attention system at that moment. But this is not what happens in perception. We are somehow able to integrate present items of attention with items from the immediate past in order to form a more complex and unified present perception. We can review the immediate past *as though it were present*, and we can form therefrom a complex present perception. This happens when we look at a large object, say a nearby building, which is too big to take in at a single glance, and this also happens in a linguistic clause. In order to perceive something all at once, though it passes through our attention system bit by bit, we need to have a consolidating function that supplements our attention-monitor. We need a perceptual depository able to store perceived but not yet organized items and to keep them available on demand.

It is safe to say that the interactions between attention and this perceptual depository are not well understood. But the existence of this depository has been known to psychologists for quite a long time. In 1890 William James called it "elementary" or "primary" memory and described its essential character better than anyone since:

> What elementary memory makes us aware of is the *just* past. The objects we feel in this directly intuited past differ from properly recollected objects. An object which is recollected, in the proper sense of that term, is one which has been absent from consciousness altogether, and now revives anew. It is brought back, recalled, fished up, so to speak, from a reservoir in which, with countless other objects, it lay buried and lost from view. But an object of primary memory is not thus brought back; it never was lost; its date was never cut off in consciousness from that of the immediately present moment.

In fact it comes to us as belonging to the rearward portion of
the present space of time, and not to the genuine past. [25]

The distinction which James draws between *primary memory*
and *recollection* has proved to be a highly durable distinction
despite recent efforts to blur its boundaries. Modern psychologists
usually give the two functions the names *short-term memory* and
long-term memory, a usage I shall follow here.

Since James's time, research has uncovered some facts about
short-term memory which are highly pertinent to readability.
The basic discovery is the precisely limited capacity of short-term
memory, a limitation which appears to be more definite for the
number of items it can store than for the number of seconds
during which it can store them. The most famous and interesting
account of this limitation is Miller's article "The Magic Number
Seven, Plus or Minus Two." (More recent studies suggest that, in
language, the limitation of items in short-term memory is closer
to five than to seven.) [26] Obviously, there is a connection between
this psychological universal and the readability of clauses. If the
clause requires a reader to exceed the capacity of his short-term
memory, then the clause will not be very readable, because some
of its functional words or phrases will have been forgotten before
the clause terminates, and the reader will have to go through the
scanning-reviewing process all over again.

This general observation certainly does not imply a simple,
direct connection between clause length and readability. The
now-proved existence of such a connection merely shows that
very brief clauses don't normally tax our short-term memories, so
we don't normally have to go through the scanning-reviewing
process more than once. Yet many short clauses can be made
more readable than they are, and many long clauses can be made
highly readable by well-trained writers. Hence, the connection
between readability and short-term memory is rather complex,
and involves much more than merely the number of words in a
clause.

One of these complicating factors is the grammatical structure

25. W. James, *Principles of Psychology* (New York, 1890), 1:647.

26. See D. E. Broadbent, "The Magic Number Seven," in *Studies in Long
Term Memory*, ed. A. Kennedy and A. Wilkes (London, 1975). Miller's
pathbreaking essay of 1956 is reprinted in G. A. Miller, *The Psychology of
Communication* (New York, 1967).

of a clause. The term *structure*, being nontemporal, immediately suggests why short-term memory is essential to the processing of a temporal phenomenon like language. The grammatical structure is revealed and confirmed as the words unfold, but that nontemporal structure could not be revealed unless its unfolding components remained present to the mind. And since there is a firm limitation on the number of elements that can remain present to the mind, there is a firm limitation on the permissible complexities of grammatical structure in all languages. This principle has been ably argued in a brilliant and pathbreaking article by Victor Yngve, who uses the term *depth* for the number of relationships which any grammatical structure requires a person to keep in short-term memory. [27]

Since Yngve's argument imposes limitations on *all* grammatical systems, it has implications (which we need not consider) for the whole field of linguistic description and historical philology. For our purposes, we can focus on the relevance of grammatical "depth" to the readability of synonymous clauses. Briefly and simply conceived, grammatical depth is determined by the number of hierarchical steps that must precede semantic closure within a clause. The idea of hierarchy is a crucial idea because, as I shall illustrate, a given number of elements operating on the same grammatical plane will be much less taxing to short-term memory than an equal number of elements in a grammatical hierarchy.

The idea of hierarchy, as I use it here, corresponds to "depth" in Yngve's phrasing but commends itself as a more descriptive term than "depth" for the temporal, psychological process whereby we *build up* meaning in reading a clause. Here is one of Yngve's examples:

a certainly not very clearly defined color

The usual way to show its grammatical structure is by a branching diagram:

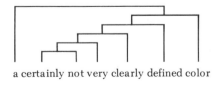

a certainly not very clearly defined color

27. V. Yngve, "A Model and an Hypothesis for Language Structure," *Proceedings of the American Philosophical Society* 104 (1960): 444–66.

The pattern of the diagram is currently called "left-branching" by theorists, but Yngve's term "regressive" is more descriptive psychologically, because the mind must always go back to a previous element or complex of elements before it grasps the present element.

The hierarchical nature of the structure can be shown by another sort of picture:

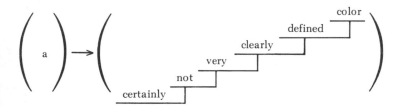

The phrase can be made less taxing to memory, as Yngve shows, by rearranging the sequence:

certainly not a very clearly defined color

which he structures thus:

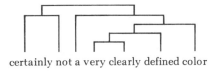

certainly not a very clearly defined color

This different hierarchy requires less memory load, as can be shown in the following picture:

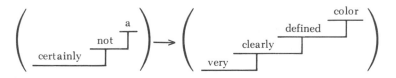

The somewhat arbitrary brackets in this revised picture bring out the psychological reality of phrase units, a reality well-attested to by data on hesitations and intonation breaks in speech.[28] The

28. D. S. Boomer, "Hesitation and Grammatical Encoding," *Language and Speech* 8 (1965): 148–58; E. Martin, "Toward an Analysis of Subjective Phrase Structure," *Psychological Bulletin* 74 (1970): 153–66.

brackets, which correspond roughly to intonation breaks, are inserted in the model to suggest a partial semantic closure. The closure of the first phrase is imperfect because it requires a further completion, as the arrow suggests. Yet the elements within the brackets function as an already processed semantic unit, thus reducing the number of items suspended in short-term memory.

That such a picture is psychologically descriptive in a rough way is confirmed when we examine "progressive" or "right-branching" diagrams. Here is another example from Yngve:

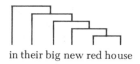

in their big new red house

Visually, that looks just as deep as:

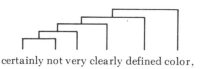

certainly not very clearly defined color,

The only visual difference between the two structures is that the steps move in different directions. But the grammatical suspensions in short-term memory are much fewer in the progressive structure for the same number of words.

$$\left(\; in\; \right) \longrightarrow \left(\; \underset{their}{\underbrace{\quad big\ new\ red\quad}}\overset{house}{\quad}\; \right)$$

Here, although the number of lexical items is the same, the number of hierarchical relations suspended in memory is much reduced. In the color phrase there were five subordinates, while in the phrase about the big red house there are just one or possibly two grammatical subordinations. Now, each step in a grammatical hierarchy is an item suspended in short-term memory, an item which has to be superadded to other lexical-semantic items suspended in short-term memory. This means that a regressive, or truly hierarchical, structure puts a greater load on short-term memory than does a progressive, or planar, structure, and it also means that more items must be processed by the central monitor.

The fact that Yngve depth does increase processing time has been known for some time.[29] Recently, Forster and Ryder have supplied evidence "that hypotheses about sense and syntax are pursued serially," supporting the view that memory load is increased by the grammatical suspensions of a regressive, hierarchical structure.[30]

These grammatical considerations have an important but complex application to the readability of clauses. Common sense instructs us that readability is not always effectively enhanced when we simply reduce grammatical subordinations. Under certain conditions, the communication of meaning is *improved* by hierarchical constructions, as Rommetveit showed in the following experiment.[31] Subjects were asked to identify one of 16 curved lines after hearing a verbal description of the target curve. The following two descriptions were used:

A leftward, jaggedly descending broken curve.
A jagged, broken curve, descending leftward.

These have roughly the following structures:

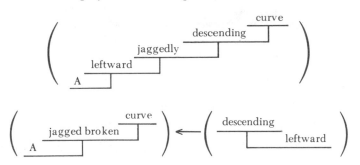

While the second description is less hierarchical, and thus easier to process, its meaning was in fact conveyed less successfully. Rommetveit conjectures that the greater effectiveness of the first description is owing to its greater cohesiveness. "A splitting up of

29. See P. N. Johnson-Laird, "Experimental Psycholinguistics," *Annual Review of Psychology* 25 (1974): 135–60. This is an excellent review article covering recent work in language processing.

30. K. I. Forster and L. A. Ryder, "Perceiving the Structure and Meaning of Sentences," *Journal of Verbal Learning and Verbal Behavior* 10 (1971): 285–96.

31. R. Rommetveit, *Words, Meanings, and Messages* (New York, 1968), pp. 287–300.

the adjectives such that some appear before and others after the noun seems to make for more decoding stations along the temporal axis of the utterance, and hence for an organization of the composite cognitions into particular substructures."[32]

This explanation rings true. It says, in effect, that the second version divides into two partial semantic units, whereas the first must be processed as a single integrated unit. The second version is easier to process initially because each of its two parts is less taxing to short-term memory. But the second version is harder to integrate into a single, semantically closed unit. This is another illustration of the conflict that consistently arises between the factors that help determine readability. Again, we are led to the view that good stylistic choices are based upon intelligent compromises between conflicting psychological factors.

I enter this caveat, which points again to the last section of this chapter, in order to forestall premature inferences about the relations of readability and grammatical form. Nonetheless, the description of the jagged, broken curve is an extreme case, which must not divert attention from the far more important principles of reducing local uncertainty and reducing the load on short-term memory. Another experiment cited by Rommetveit strikingly illustrates the superior importance of these two principles. Groups of subjects were given one of the following two verbal descriptions:

    I. A secretary who is severe, cool, extraordinary, beautiful, pleasant.
   II. A severe, cool, extraordinary, beautiful, pleasant secretary.

More than *twice* as many adjectives were given back after description I than after description II. Semantic closure was achieved after each adjective in description I, but not until the end in description II. In general, we must conclude that readability is greatly enhanced by speedy, even though partial, semantic closures within a clause. By this method, semantic uncertainty and memory load will be small even in rather lengthy clauses.

Is there, in fact, a relationship between memory load and uncertainty within a clause? The intuitive answer is "yes," and it is undoubtedly the right answer. The function of the short-term memory bank is to store and to offer up on demand any partly

32. Ibid., p. 300.

processed element of the clause. Its ability to do this is limited by the number of elements which it is able to hold. If the number of elements gets too big, some of them get forgotten, and the reader has to look again. But the number of elements held in short-term memory is *not* determined by the mere number of preceding words in the clause. For example, in the following reordering of Yngve's color-phrase, the reader must still process all the words up to the very end:

a color certainly not defined very clearly

The reordered phrase is easier mainly because the elements are "unitized" (to use George Miller's term):

(a color)← (certainly not defined)← (very clearly)

All of the words are in short-term memory right up to *clearly*, but, because the words are grouped in partly closed semantic-syntactic units, these *groups* rather than the individual words are held in suspension. The advantages to short-term memory of such "unitizing" or "chunking" has been proved conclusively. [33] At the last word of the reordered phrase (i.e., *clearly*), memory has in storage only about two elements rather than four or five, even though it still holds in storage the same number of words.

This consideration helps explain the relationship between uncertainty and memory load. Uncertainty works against memory in two ways. By increasing the number of meaning-candidates being considered, it increases the time which memory must hold elements in storage. But the more important conflict between memory and uncertainty is the tendency of uncertainty to prevent partial closure within the clause. If, for instance, we increased the uncertainty of Yngve's example, we might get this:

a certainly not again nearly designed color

The chief reason for the great memory load of this phrase is not the delay created by reviewing many more semantic-syntactic candidates, though that delay should not be underestimated. The main burden on the memory is the failure of the words to form themselves in stable groups. Many of them have to be re-membered as individual words rather than as phrases, thereby greatly increasing the number of elements held in storage.

33. G. A. Miller, *The Psychology of Communication* (Harmondsworth, 1970), chap. 2.

If this conjecture about the conflict between memory and uncertainty should prove to be correct, it would explain rather precisely the correlation between predictability and readability. If every word-sequence in the clause is functioning according to expectations, the reader is constantly forming the word-sequences into stable groups which do not need to be revised. The functions of the word-groups may be somewhat indefinite until the clause is complete, but if the groupings are stable, the burden on short-term memory will remain small. And if the groupings are both stable and progressive (in Yngve's sense), then memory will be burdened least of all. Moreover, since the normalization of syntax and spelling is a way of insuring the stability of provisional groupings of words, this explanation of the connection between uncertainty and memory fits in well with the known historical facts about the readability of prose.

One of these historical facts has been the decline of the periodic sentence, and the obvious explanation for its decline is that it tends to put too great a strain on short-term memory. On the other hand, the really interesting feature of the periodic sentence is its degree of readability in the hands of a good writer. To find an example, one can turn to any page of Macaulay's early prose. (His later style advanced to greater simplicity.) Here is a fairly short example from the essay on Dryden (1828):

> Of Dryden however, as of almost every man who has been
> distinguished either in the literary or in the political world,
> it may be said that the course which he pursued and the effect
> which he produced, depended less on his personal qualities
> than on the circumstances in which he was placed.

Such a sentence is readable because it creaks with devices of predictability, making every first guess about word groupings the right guess:

> Of Dryden
> as of almost every man
> distinguished
> in the literary or ⎫
> in the political ⎭ world
> it may be said

At this point closure is quite complete, as one can see, when the phrase *it may be said* is changed to *this may be said* (:), and a new sentence is started. Moreover, every short-term expectancy is fulfilled, and every rhythmical, syntactic, and even alliterative pattern is continued. All writers of successful periodic sentences, no matter how long these are, strictly delimit the strain on the reader's short-term memory. They do this by subclausal groupings and by intrasentence groupings which have the effective semantic closure of complete sentences. A good, long periodic sentence is, in effect, a paragraph. Its semantic cohesion goes beyond that of the clause and enters the domain of long-term memory.

That is why a good periodic sentence is a phenomenon very different from, say, a long dependent clause in German, which requires that the verb be withheld until the end. This German phenomenon deserves mention because it *does* put a strain upon short-term memory, and under Darwinian (Zipfian) linguistic conditions should therefore have become extinct. Unquestionably, the verb-at-the-end rule would have been banished from all long clauses in German if the language planners of the seventeenth and eighteenth centuries had not permanently imposed their views of correctness on the German language. Earlier German dependent clauses—in the Luther Bible, for instance— characteristically put the verb in the middle, just as in independent clauses. In the present day, the verb-at-the-end rule holds in none of the oral dialects of German. It is a psychological and linguistic dinosaur preserved only in the rules of the German grapholect, much to the detriment of that language as an effective instrument of prose.

In sum, the crucial concept in the readability of clauses is the concept of closure—whether partial, as in phrases, or complete, as in sentence-clauses. Readability is enhanced when closure is rapid and stable, since rapid and stable closure greatly reduces both processing time and the burden on short-term memory.

Semantic Integration and Long-Term Memory

What makes single clauses easy to process is now fairly well understood because experiments on single clauses can be set up very precisely and retested by psychologists all over the world. But experiments with connected prose are much harder to set up, and their variables are very difficult to keep under control. Hence, the tendency of current empirical research is to go on refining our knowledge of sentence-, clause-, and word-processing rather than our understanding of the psycholinguistic principles which connect clauses with one another in extended discourse. The onward march of prose is assumed to be a continual processing of single sentences, which, after being understood, are consigned to an uncharted ocean called "long-term memory."

This current way of regarding prose is exemplified in Bever's model of speech perception: "(1) The clause is the primary perceptual unit; (2) within each clause we assign semantic relations between major phrases; (3) after each clause is processed, it is recoded into a relatively abstract form, thereby leaving short-term memory available for processing the next clause."[34] While this model is undoubtedly correct and follows the pattern I outlined in the preceding section, the model has nothing to say about the linkages between the clause that is now being processed and earlier clauses which have already passed into memory, "recoded into a relatively abstract form." On Bever's model, our attention turns ever again to the next clause rather than to its integration with earlier discourse. Yet that unmapped frontier where we connect present and past linguistic perceptions is obviously a subject of very great interest for the psychology of prose. It is this frontier which largely determines the readability of prose discourse, as distinct from the readability of its individual sentences.

The movement of the mind from present perceptions to long-term memory, and then the subsequent retrieval from long-term memory back to present perception, embraces almost the whole domain of cognitive psychology. My strategy for dealing with this immense and disputed realm will be, as before, a strategy of narrowing the focus to those elements which play a role in the readability of prose. By this means, I can avoid premature commitment to any particular psychological model and can stress instead certain interesting experiments on extended discourse which bear directly on this larger dimension of readability. More specifically, I shall stress the factors which help to link a clause that is being processed with the earlier clauses that have already been "recoded" abstractly in long-term memory.

In essence, the problem of easing the psychological links between clauses is similar to the problem of easing semantic

34. Bever, "Perception, Thought and Language," in Carroll and Freedle, *Language Comprehension and the Acquistition of Knowledge*, p. 104.

integration within the clause. In both cases, the aim is to achieve a speedy and easy transformation of sequential verbal elements into a nonsequential *structure* of meaning. First, within the clause, the aim is to structure a sequence of words into phrases and then a sequence of phrases into a clause. In order to perform this feat, our working memory must hold in suspension an array of items until they have been formed into a closed semantic structure—the clause or sentence. Similarly, for a series of clauses, the aim is to achieve a speedy and easy integration of the ongoing clauses into still larger nonsequential structures of meaning. Although this model is rather schematic, we cannot doubt that one way of facilitating the perception of extended discourse (that is, of enhancing readability) is to facilitate the integration of temporal clause-sequences into nontemporal structures of meaning.

In discourse, this accommodating of the temporal to the nontemporal was first described by a great early psychologist, St. Augustine:

> I am about to repeat a psalm that I know. Before I begin,
> my expectation alone extends all at once over the whole: but
> as soon as I have begun, however much of it I shall carry into
> the past, over that much my memory now extends. So the life
> of this action of mine extends both ways—into my memory,
> for that part which I have already repeated, and into my ex-
> pectation, for that part which I am about to repeat. But all
> this while, my marking faculty is present at hand, and by its
> means that which was future is conveyed over that it may
> become past. So that, while this marking faculty continues to
> to work diligently, the expectation is shortened and the
> memory enlarged, until the whole expectation at length
> vanishes, and the whole action now ended, shall be altogether
> passed into the memory. What is now done in this whole
> psalm, the same is done also in every part of it, yea and in
> every syllable of it. [35]

What Augustine depicts is a paradox that embraces both the pro-duction and reception of speech. On either side of the temporal sequence of discourse is a nontemporal expected meaning and a nontemporal remembered meaning, unified with each other and somehow integrated with the ongoing perceptual (or productive) process.

35. *The Confessions*, Book XI.

Before turning to those traits of discourse which facilitate this integration, I shall describe some post-Augustinian research which lends impressive support to Augustine's nontemporal, hence nonsyntactic model of semantic memory. Some decisive experimentation in this field was reported as long ago (or as recently!) as 1894, in a classic paper by Binet and Henri. [36] They discovered that when children were asked to recall short, eleven word passages they *could* remember the syntactic and lexical form of the utterances; but, when asked to recall longer passages of sixty to eighty-six words, they remembered the meaning accurately but not the form. Our memory of unrehearsed discourse is short-lived, but our memory of discourse *meaning* (recoded in memory in an abstract, nonverbal form) is highly durable. Put another way, after a linguistic clause has been processed, it is stored in a nonlinguistic, nonsequential form.

Beginning in 1966, this old discovery has been refined and reconfirmed several times, and its principal implications are no longer seriously in doubt. But because these findings run against certain widespread suppositions in linguistics and literary theory, it will be useful to describe briefly the experimental results. In 1966, Fillenbaum reported that subjects in recognition tests were poor in detecting substitutions such as *closed* for *not open*. [37] In 1967, Sachs found that after twelve seconds her subjects could not recognize whether the original sentence was in the active or the passive voice, although their memory for meaning was excellent. [38] In 1970, Johnson-Laird reported a significantly unsuccessful experiment designed to discover the locus of the tendency for passives to be recalled as actives:

> In the event, the promised phenomenon did not materialize. When the subjects were confronted with an unexpected test of their ability to recognize the sentences of a brief spoken story, they recalled actives as passives just as often as they recalled passives as actives. Yet their memory for meaning was extremely good.

On the basis of these results, Johnson-Laird stated: "all forms of syntactic structure are normally lost to memory within a few

36. A. Binet, and V. Henri, "La mémoire des phrases (mémoire des idées)," *Année psychologique* 1 (1894): 24–59.

37. S. Fillenbaum, "Memory for Gist: Some Relevant Variables," *Language and Speech* 9 (1966): 217–27.

38. J. S. Sachs, "Recognition Memory for Syntactic and Semantic Aspects of Connected Discourse," *Perception and Psychophysics* 2 (1967): 437–42.

seconds.... No one knows how meaning is represented within memory, but there is no evidence to show that any form of syntactic structure is directly involved." [39]

Since Johnson-Laird's summary, the evidence for his view has continued to pile up. In their review of 1975, Levelt and Kempen express doubt that the implicit assumption of earlier linguistic work can now be maintained—"namely the presupposition that what is stored in memory is some sort of linguistic object." [40] The capstone to this work is an interesting set of experiments, conducted by Brewer, on the tendency of people to recall a synonym of the original word instead of the word itself. [41] These experiments decisively exclude the possibility that clauses are normally stored in memory either as linguistic traces or as images. These interesting and, taken together, decisive results have implications going far beyond the problem of semantic integration in prose, but I must not digress.

The experimental results suggest that we integrate current meanings with our semantic memory of the whole discourse mainly at the transition points between clauses. For only at these transitions are we still accurately remembering the verbal features of the preceding clause. These transitions are crucial because we normally have only about twelve seconds to make secure verbal links between a completed clause and the one being processed. After twelve seconds, our memory for linguistic form begins to decay and becomes increasingly insecure as the delay gets longer. [42]

From these data alone, we can make some relevant inferences about how to write good prose. Since the meaning of the whole discourse (remembered and expected) is mainly stored in a nontemporal, nonlinguistic form, the writer will assist the reader by continually repeating a rather small number of thematic tags which *represent* that remembered (and expected) holistic mean-

39. P. N. Johnson-Laird, "The Perception and Memory of Sentences," in *New Horizons in Linguistics*, ed. J. Lyons (Harmondsworth, 1970), pp. 261–70.

40. W. J. M. Levelt and G. Kempen, "Semantic and Syntactic Aspects of Remembering Sentences: A Review of Some Recent Continental Research," in *Studies in Long Term Memory*, ed. A. Kennedy and A. Wilkes (London, 1975), pp. 201–18.

41. W. F. Brewer, "Memory for Ideas: Synonym Substitution," *Memory and Cognition* 3 (1975): 458–64. See also W. Kintsch, *The Representation of Meaning in Memory* (Hillsdale, New Jersey, 1974), passim.

42. Sachs, "Recognition Memory for Syntactic and Semantic Aspects of Connected Discourse," pp. 437–42.

ing. If the thematic tags are too numerous, they cannot be held at once in working memory, and in that case the whole meaning will seem disconnected and incoherent. A second inference, on the smaller scale, is that the transition points between clauses can aid semantic integration if they contain words which *specify* a semantic connection between the current clause and the preceding one.

Fortunately, we do have at last some empirical confirmation of these deductions. But before I describe these data, I want to expatiate briefly on the idea of using only a few thematic tags to represent the complex, larger meanings of a discourse. This inference is so susceptible to misunderstanding that I had better defend it now rather than defer that task to the final chapter. What I say might seem to elevate a particular sort of repetitive style above all others, and I would have certainly deferred discussion of such a practical inference except that a very fundamental psychological principle is involved.

It is the principle of *representation*. Cassirer made this principle central to his linguistical-epistemological speculations, and his introductory remarks on representation are among the best parts of his *Philosophy of Symbolic Forms*. The psychological device of representation is the principal device of the mind for coping with complex wholes of all sorts. Instead of trying to think about a whole meaning in its complex fullness and in its relation to other complexities, we isolate a part (or we use a short symbol) in order to represent the whole. By this means, we can deal easily and simply with complexities that we otherwise could not possibly attend to all at once. Hence representation is not just a device to facilitate the integration of meaning in prose; it is an essential device of all complex thought.

What I have called a *thematic tag* is an explicit verbal representation of many implicit meanings. The tag is the visible part of a semantic iceberg. We cannot write or speak without making use of such representational tags. Even the most explicit legal document uses terms whose exact implicit meanings reside in a long tradition of legal interpretation. A legal tag like *per stirpes*, for instance, represents this tradition of legal interpretation as an implication of the tag's use in a legal document. Similarly, in a psychological text, the phrase *short-term memory* is used as a thematic tag for a complex system of mental functions which needn't be described in each use. In a novel, the mere name of a character, say *James Bond*, is a thematic tag for an elaborate system of character traits that needn't be rehearsed every time *Bond* is used in a sentence. And so on, for all kinds of words in all kinds of texts. Representation by thematic tags is absolutely essential to language use because of our limited capacity for paying attention to several explicit meanings all at once. Only by representation, and hence by thematic tags, can we accommodate our limited storage capacity, during an on-going temporal discourse, to our very large capacity in long-term memory for nontemporal structures of meaning.

The importance of representation by thematic tags is well illustrated in some very recent work on the psychology of prose conducted by Walter Kintsch and his colleagues. Kintsch's work seems to me the best and most promising work on extended discourse to be found in the psychological literature, and its results to date powerfully reinforce my deductions about the main factors that affect the semantic integration of prose. In 1973, Kintsch and Keenan reported that, with prose passages of equal length and equal word- and sentence-difficulty, both reading rate and retention could be predicted from a quantitative analysis of content. [43] Their special form of content analysis consisted of counting the number of propositions in the passages according to a shrewdly designed system for identifying the propositions. The experiments showed that, with other factors kept under control, reading time increased an average of 1.5 seconds for each additional proposition in passages of the same length. The experiments also showed better retention for main propositions than for subordinate ones.

These data were conceived to be preparatory to more informative experiments. One of the chief results of this preliminary work was to demonstrate the feasibility and reliability of textual proposition-counting, according to the system devised by Kintsch. A later report, issued in 1975, showed results of far greater consequence and subtlety. [44] This report was based on a number of different experiments conducted on different kinds of prose texts: short and long texts from history books, and short and long texts from *Scientific American*. Since the results were consistent in all cases, I shall summarize them en masse.

The chief novelty of the experimentation was the idea of

43. W. Kintsch and J. Keenan, "Reading Rate and Retention as a Function of the Number of Propositions in the Base Structure of Sentences," *Cognitive Psychology* 5 (1973): 257–74.

44. W. Kintsch et al., "Comprehension and Recall of Text as a Function of Content Variables," *Journal of Verbal Learning and Verbal Behavior* 14 (1975): 196–214.

keeping constant the number of propositions and the passage lengths but changing the number of word concepts (i.e., thematic tags) used to express the same number of propositions. The results in all cases were highly pertinent to the semantic integration and readability of prose. Wherever the same number of propositions were expressed with fewer thematic tags, the subject not only read the passages faster but recalled more of the propositions.[45] The most dramatic and also the most accurate quantification of these results is found by correlating the reading times with the number of propositions recalled, as in table 1.

Table 1. Mean Number of Seconds of
Reading Time per Proposition Recalled

Paragraph Length and Subject		Few Tags per Proposition	Many Tags per Proposition (% increase)	
Short	History	1.73 secs.	2.13 secs.	(+239%)
	Science	1.45	2.97	(+105%)
Long	History	1.62	2.03	(+25%)
	Science	2.74	3.80	(+39%)

If one takes the median of these percentage increases, one gets a striking 32 percent increase in reading time per proposition recalled for passages that use relatively many thematic tags to represent the same number of propositions.

To illustrate the kind of contrasts used in the experiments, here are two passages of similar lengths, containing eight propositions. The first uses only three thematic tags, while the second uses eight.

1. The Greeks loved beautiful art. When the Romans conquered the Greeks, they copied them, and thus learned to create beautiful art. (21 words, 8 propositions)
2. The Babylonians built a beautiful garden on a hill. They planted lovely flowers, constructed fountains and designed a pavilion for the queen's pleasure. (23 words, 8 propositions)

In order to show that the two passages do indeed express the same

45. By "number" of thematic tags in discourse, I mean the number of *different* tags. A few tags, repeated many times, will increase readability, while many tags, repeated few times, will decrease readability.

number of propositions, Kintsch provided the following schematic analysis:

I. Greek Art Passage
   Propositions
   1 (LOVE, GREEK, ART)
   2   (BEAUTIFUL, ART)
   3   (CONQUER, ROMAN, GREEK)
   4   (COPY, ROMAN, GREEK)
   5   (WHEN, 3, 4)
   6   (LEARN, ROMAN, 8)
   7   (CONSEQUENCE, 3, 6)
   8   (CREATE, ROMAN, 2)

Arguments (i.e., thematic tags): GREEK, ART, ROMAN. The arabic numbers inside the parentheses represent repetitions of propositions by means of the original thematic tags for them.

II. Babylonian Passage
    Propositions
    1 (BUILD, BABYLONIAN, GARDEN)
    2   (BEAUTIFUL, GARDEN)
    3   (LOCATION: ON, GARDEN, HILL)
    4   (PLANT, BABYLONIAN, FLOWER)
    5   (LOVELY, FLOWER)
    6   (CONSTRUCT, BABYLONIAN, FOUNTAIN)
    7   (DESIGN, BABYLONIAN, PAVILION, 8)
    8   (HAS, QUEEN, PLEASURE)

Arguments (thematic tags): BABYLONIAN, HILL, GARDEN, FLOWER, FOUNTAIN, PAVILION, QUEEN, PLEASURE. In this passage, only one proposition (no. 7) contains a new proposition that repeats an earlier thematic tag.

A better indicator of the phenomenon described in this research would be a comparison of synonymous passages which differed only in the number of thematic tags. I hope that such experimentation will be carried out.[46] Meanwhile, here is my own rendering of such a contrast. I shall take the first letter-to-the-editor in today's college paper. It begins as follows:

To the editor.

Dear Sir:

The article in yesterday's issue has prompted us to offer a clarification of our actions. We hope to eliminate any confusion

46. Kintsch has, in fact, made a start on such research. See Kintsch, *The Representation of Meaning in Memory*, pp. 107–22.

which might have developed as a result of the strong similarity between our campaign literature and that used by the current administration in last year's election [47 words]

Here is a revision that reduces the number of thematic tags without reducing the number of propositions or changing the number of words.

To the editor.

Dear Sir:

Your article, published yesterday, demonstrated a strong similarity between the wording of our campaign literature and the wording of the campaign literature used by the winners of last year's election. Publication of your article now prompts us to explain why we used similar wording in our campaign [47 words]

The reader will have to make his own subjective judgment about the probable correlations of reading-time with propositions remembered in these two passages.

This kind of example illustrates one of the principal techniques for easing semantic integration between clauses. By reducing the number of thematic tags in a clause sequence the writer accomplishes two integrative functions: first, he reduces the load on short-term memory so that the discourse can be conceived as unified when the reader pays attention to the clause sequence as a whole; second, the writer links the clauses together by repeating verbal tags in contiguous clauses. These activities—reducing the number of thematic tags and repeating the tags in contiguous clauses—tend, of course, to be corollary.

The second principal technique in facilitating semantic integration between clauses is to provide explicit verbal links which express the principal semantic connections between clauses. Such words as *similarly, nonetheless, thus, but, and, moreover, however, on the other hand, secondly*, are explicit verbal links which assist integration by forecasting the relationship between the ongoing clause and the preceding one. Such words function prospectively for the clause being processed and also retrospectively for clauses already stored. Integration, is similarly enhanced by using purely prospective devices such as showing in advance the nature of the clauses to follow, that is, showing whether they will be a series of similarities, a set of contrasts, a rhythmical pattern, and so on. This forecasting helps to integrate clauses with one another and, by reducing uncertainty, also serves to speed up the processing of individual clauses.

These considerations will seem familiar to composition teachers, whether or not they have pondered their psychological foundations. In my own case, the exposure to psychological research has clarified the old composition trinity, *unity, coherence,* and *emphasis.* All three qualities are enhanced by the reduction of thematic tags and the use of prospective-retrospective links. While this manner of describing the old shibboleth does leave out of account questions of large-scale organization and of paragraphing, it covers, I believe, all of the most important truths in the doctrine of unity, coherence, and emphasis. [47]

The main objection to thematic tags and prospective links is their apparent artificiality. Since ordinary speech does not have to contextualize and canalize discourse within the verbal medium alone, ordinary speech achieves semantic integration without using special integrative devices. The most obvious answer to the charge of artificiality is that writing itself is inherently artificial, if one takes ordinary speech as the norm. Artificiality is natural to writing. Untutored composition, when it lacks devices of semantic integration, seems inept, cumbersome, and artificial.

But an even stronger argument for the canalization of discourse through integrative devices is the argument for the necessity of representation within all speech and thought. Integration is enhanced by using a small number of representational *surface* semantic units. But this does not in itself deplete the richness of subsurface implications. If, as Cassirer argues, representation is the soul of speech, then the unsaid is always completing the said. The true danger in reducing the explicit, surface thematic tags of prose is the danger of leaving too much unsaid. When that happens the reader will not understand enough about the underside of the iceberg. Here again we find a conflict between ease of processing and security of communication, and once again we find that good prose requires an intelligent compromise between conflicting psychological factors.

Reconciling Conflicts of Readability

Even if a writer wanted to achieve maximum readability at the expense of all other considerations, he would fail if he merely followed a simple formula. If all his clauses were short and all his

47. A good discussion of emphasis from a psycholinguistic standpoint can be found in M. A. K. Halliday, "Language Structure and Language Function," in *New Horizons in Linguistics*, ed. J. Lyons (Harmondsworth, 1970), pp. 140–65.

words familiar; if he used only the active voice and avoided using negatives; if he stuck to just a few thematic tags and bound his sentences each to each with *but, moreover,* and *thus*; if he focused the reader's attention on a single main idea in every paragraph and made his words fall into place in a predictable rhythm, he would still fail to achieve maximum readability. The net effect of his writing would be monotony. His repetitive style would fatigue the attention of his reader, whose mind would wander to other affairs in search of relief from the boredom of the text. Instead of increasing readability, the end result of following simple readability rules would be to increase rather than decrease processing time. Moreover, even if the writer added another rule, "avoid monotony," his basic formula would still fail him, since he would then have to introduce rare words, long clauses, passive voices, negatives, thematic variations, and shifts of rhythm, all in opposition to his basic formula. So, even if he ruthlessly excluded every other aim in favor of readability, the writer would still have to make intelligent compromises among conflicting principles.

The importance of stylistic compromise will be greater still when the writer also has something to say, and therefore cares less for readability than for adequacy of communication. The recurrent (though not inevitable) conflict between readability and communicative adequacy prompted me earlier to introduce the concept of *relative* readability as a central concept of this book. I shall end this chapter by discussing relative readability in psychological terms. Earlier, in Chapter 4, I defined relative readability as a function of the writer's semantic intentions. Here, I want to discuss the typical conflicts between semantic intention and ease of processing, with a view to formulating a general principle for resolving the conflicts.

Probably the most basic conflict is between rapidity of closure and adequacy of conveyed meaning. Obviously, the following is easier to read than its original by Abraham Lincoln:

Eighty-seven years ago our fathers founded a
nation based on freedom and equality.

What is missing from this is intuitively known to every person familiar with the "Gettysburg Address." The "propositions" are the same as Lincoln's, but the meaning is inadequate to Lincoln's semantic intentions, which probably included: biblical majesty of utterance ("fourscore and seven years ago"); the implication that this nation is like a living being (it was "conceived," "brought forth," and its life was "dedicated" to a principle). If these implications and semantic effects were not part of Lincoln's aim, then of course the revision, being shorter even than Lincoln's compact utterance, would be superior.

Having started with this example, I cannot refrain from observing digressively how brilliantly Lincoln's whole speech follows the psychological principles I have been discussing in this chapter. Each phrase group is understood as a unit that requires no mental revision. Each clause unfolds progressively (in Yngve's sense). No phrasal unit is so long that it burdens the memory before the clause is closed. The longest phrasal interruption between a verb and its object is about three words, as in

brought forth [on this continent] a new nation.

An apparent exception is really no exception at all:

We can not dedicate—
we can not consecrate—
we can not hallow—
this ground.

because the single object of these verbs was already known from the closely preceding sentence: "We have come to dedicate a portion of that field." Moreover, the repetition of thematic tags assures that the connections between the sentences will be attended to and remembered (in the following list of tags, I have not even recorded synonyms and cognates):

sentence 1: nation conceived dedicated,
sentence 2: we war, nation conceived, dedicated
sentence 3: we field, war
sentence 4: we, dedicate field, nation
sentence 5: we do this
sentence 6: we dedicate, consecrate, ground
sentence 7: consecrated ground, dead, living
sentence 8: fought, we
sentence 9: for us dedicated, living, fought
sentence 10: for us, dedicated, dead, nation

Lincoln's devices of semantic integration could be described with much more detail and subtlety, but I shall avoid further digression from my present subject of reconciling conflicting forces.

The most important conflicts within the domain of readability may be summarized in two oppositions, both of which set processing speed against meaning. By processing speed I mean speed of closure. It is the speed with which a phrase, clause, sentence, or even a paragraph is processed as a semantic unit by the reader and then stored in his long-term memory. Taking speed of closure as a universal factor in readability, the two main conflicts are:

(1) speed of closure vs. semantic integration
and
(2) speed of closure vs. semantic adequacy.

Both oppositions are crucial to the concept of relative readability, because the semantic element in each opposition indicates the relativity of reading ease to semantic intentions.

Speed of closure vs. semantic integration. This opposition first appeared in the surprising result, reported by Rommetveit, that a single, memory-taxing description may be better unified in memory than two shorter and more speedily closed descriptions. His example was:

A leftward, jaggedly descending broken curve,

which was better remembered than:

A jagged, broken curve, descending leftward.

I wonder, though, what his results would have been if he had followed the pattern of his *secretary* sentence, and had substituted the following description instead:

A jagged, broken curve that goes down to the left.

It is possible that his results might have been very different. I think they would have been. My longer, revised version has substituted a *that* clause for an *ing* phrase. One effect of this substitution is that a clear boundary is formed (marked by *that*) between the two semantically closed parts of the curve description. This boundary unites by dividing. The mind does not have to reverse direction at the boundary because the word *that* informs the reader in advance that more is to come about the curve. The importance of this advance information has been shown in experiments which compare the processing of two otherwise identical sentences, one with and one without an explicit *who* or *which* coming before a relative clause; and also in experiments which compare "complement constructions" with or without a preceding *that*. In each case, an explicit use of the marking word makes uptake faster, easier, and more durable.[48]

48. J. A. Fodor and M. Garrett, "Some Reflections on Competence and Performance," in *Psycholinguistic Papers*, ed. J. Lyons and R. Wales (Edinburgh, 1966), pp. 26–47; D. T. Hakes and H. S. Cairns, "Sentence Comprehen-

If these reflections on the curve experiment are correct, it follows that speed and semantic integration are not always in conflict. Indeed, I would be willing to bet that my proposed revision, though longer, will be processed faster than either of the descriptions in Rommetveit's experiment. A more characteristic conflict between speed and integration shows up when we contrast the speed of several short clauses with the integrative effect of one long clause. Here is a contrived example:

Thomas Jefferson wrote the Declaration of Independence. He is to be depicted on one side of the new two-dollar bill that will be issued by the U.S. Treasury. On the other side will be shown the scene of the signing of the Declaration. The new bill will be issued on April 13, 1976. Jefferson was born on that date in 1743. Also on April 13, 1976, the Rotunda at the University of Virginia will be reopened. Jefferson designed the Rotunda. When it burnt down almost a century ago, rebuilders failed to follow Jefferson's plans. The new reconstruction attempts to follow them precisely. The new reconstruction cost several million dollars.

This writing misses many obvious opportunities of integration. But here is what happens when a large number of these opportunities are realized all at once:

Thomas Jefferson, author of the Declaration of Independence is depicted on one side, while the signing of the Declaration is depicted on the other side, of a new two-dollar bill to be issued by the U.S. Treasury this April 13, Jefferson's birthday (in 1743) and also the date on which the Rotunda of the University of Virginia, designed by Jefferson, will be reopened after a reconstruction that cost several million dollars and which followed exactly Jefferson's original plans, unlike the previous reconstruction, which failed to follow Jefferson's plans, when the reconstruction was undertaken after the Rotunda burnt down almost a century ago.

Employing so many devices of integration to link one clause with another has the paradoxical effect of disunity rather than unity. One cause of this is that thematic changes (e.g., from the two-dollar bill to the Rotunda) are unmarked by any sentence pauses to signal the shift of theme. The reader's orientation and

sion and Relative Pronouns," *Perception and Psychophysics* 8 (1970): 5–8; D. T. Hakes, "Effects of Reducing Complement Constructions on Sentence Comprehension," *Journal of Verbal Learning and Verbal Behavior* 11 (1972): 278–86.

hence his semantic integration would be enhanced if a new sentence were started at this point: "Jefferson's birthday will also be celebrated at the University of Virginia. There, the Rotunda, designed by Jefferson, will be reopened. . . ." A new beginning at a new theme is a signpost that helps the reader to relate one theme with another and hence to integrate the meanings more securely in memory without reviewing the meanings in order to sort out the relationships. Syntactic-semantic pauses assist semantic integration in such cases. Too few pauses can cause fragmentation of meaning almost as readily as too many pauses. By making compromises between the two extremes, one can create a number of versions superior in readability to either of the extreme examples quoted above.

But the most important compromise that the writer is called upon to make for the sake of readability is a compromise between *speed of closure and semantic adequacy.* In solving this stylistic problem, the writer has to consider both the impediments inherent in his meaning and those in his audience. If his meaning is complex and subtle, he cannot always convey it with rapidly closed and highly familiar phrasal units. And even when this rapid style might work with a small and homogeneous audience, it might baffle and confuse a large, uninitiated audience—the typical readership for writing.

If the writing problem had a single, central crux we would find it here. Readability demands rapid closure to avoid taxing the reader's short-term memory. But readability also demands explicit constraints on meaning in order to guide the reader's understanding. Every word and clause has to be adequately contextualized by other explicit words and clauses in order to secure and facilitate the reader's uptake of the intended meaning. But when these local constraints on meaning require a lot of qualifying words (as in legal writing), then closure may be delayed too long. Security of communication will then be dearly bought, since, if the reader's memory is overtaxed, he will lose the thread of meaning rather than grasp it more securely.

I will limit myself to a single illustration of the contrary evils of excessive terseness and excessive explicitness. Here, first, is an overly short version:

> No region in our times, neither the Himalayas, Antarctica, nor the moon, has excited as much fascination as the Nile.

This is underexplicit because the reader lacks sufficient clues about the common features which excite fascination. Even if the reader guesses what these are, this guessing will have taken unnecessary time and effort. But here, by contrast, is an overly explicit version of the sentence:

No mysterious and unexplored region during the nineteenth and twentieth centuries, neither the Himalayas, a mountain range in Asia with the highest mountains in the world, many of them unscaled; nor Antarctica, a huge region of snow and ice surrounding the South Pole and having the severest climate on earth; nor even the hidden side of the moon, which because of the moon's orbital pattern is always turned away from the earth, has excited quite the same fascination for explorers and armchair explorers as the uncharted regions of Africa where lie the long undiscovered sources of a river, famous since biblical times, the Nile.

Nothing is to be found in the longer version that was not implicit in the shorter. But for almost any audience beyond the seventh year of schooling, the second version gives many explicit contexts which (as the writer could safely assume) his audience already knew. Between these two extremes is the sentence that Alan Moorehead actually wrote:

No unexplored region in our times, neither the heights of the Himalayas, the Antarctic wastes, nor even the hidden side of the moon, has excited quite the same fascination as the mystery of the sources of the Nile. [49]

But what would Moorehead have done if he *had* been writing for an uneducated audience? He would have given the necessary explicit information, but he would have broken that information up into easily managed, shorter units which would not tax the reader's memory.

Communicative writing is always more explicit than ordinary talk because the writer must assume an audience whose contextual associations lie somewhere between the uncertain associations of total aliens and the nearly certain ones of close intimates. The amount of explicit semantic constraint that a writer decides to impose will depend on the amount of shared implications which he assumes in his readers, and also on the amount of leeway he is willing to allow them when they construe those implications. The more the writer can assume, the more rapidly and easily he can convey his intended meaning.

But, sometimes, the meaning itself will require a rather

49. A. Moorehead, *The White Nile* (New York, 1960), p. 1.

qualified, elaborated, and difficult style. Easy, lucid, and highly readable writing is not always within the reach of the most highly skilled stylist, nor is it always the greatest desideratum of writing. This truth is summed up very well by Brand Blanshard in his elegant book on *Philosophical Style:*

> The most unfailingly lucid writer in the history of English litera-
> ture is Macaulay, whose speeches in particular are masterpieces
> of incisive statement. The trouble is, as Augustine Birrell once
> remarked, that you cannot tell the truth in Macaulay's style. In
> satisfying his passion for clarity, he allows himself to omit shades
> and qualifications that are there in the facts but would smudge
> his sharply etched lines, if he were to put them into his picture. [50]

Blanshard here uncovers what might be called "the ethics of readability." How far should a writer compromise his semantic intentions for the sake of a readable style? Like most ethical questions, this is not subject to facile or universally valid answers. But there exists, I believe, a sound principle which can help a writer reach his own decision in a particular case. If the reader must constantly reread clauses, sentences, and paragraphs to construe the writer's meaning, he will not understand or remember that meaning very well. Too much of the reader's effort will have been devoted to construing, too little to understanding, the meaning.

This implicit principle might be called the principle of linearity. So long as the reader can process what he reads without having to circle back and reread an earlier part of the text, then the writing is linear. It is writing that has not crossed over the boundary line into unreadability. Linearity determines that boundary line, and only rarely does a writer have a communicative justification for stepping over it. Since the reader stores textual meaning mainly in nonlinguistic form, and since his memory for linguistic form begins to decay very rapidly, the only memorable feature of difficult, unlinear prose is the memory of its difficulty. Its *gist* would have been better remembered if conveyed in a linear style. Hence, a lot of obscure, unlinear writing is produced on false linguistic premises and is in fact quite unjustifiable.

The principle of linearity is nonetheless very capacious. It admits highly deliberate writing, intricate and even precious writing. It admits long periodic sentences, although it may exclude

50. B. Blanshard, *On Philosophical Style* (Manchester, England, 1954), pp. 67–68.

a series of ill-composed short sentences. There are many degrees of readability within its generous boundaries. When linearity is taken as a principle for resolving stylistic conflicts, we can conceive of this resolution as a balancing of three factors. (1) Closure must occur frequently enough to accommodate short-term memory and not interrupt the forward movement of the mind. (2) Expectation must be sufficiently fulfilled to achieve semantic integration without interrupting this forward movement. (3) Contextualization must be sufficiently explicit to indicate the contours of implication without interrupting the forward movement. Adequate closure, adequate constraint, and adequate integration: these ingredients of linearity should be balanced against each other so that none is altogether neglected. Linear prose is not always easy prose, but linearity is a minimal requirement of communicative prose.

6   **Some Practical Implications**

Some Practical Implications

The Goals of Composition
in the Curriculum

Everyone accepts literacy as a goal of schooling, but the planners of school curricula are not always sure just where the skill of writing should be taught. Should it be connected with literary instruction in classes on poetry and fiction? Or should it be kept with the humbler language arts of spelling and punctuation? This sort of question gets asked at every level of education. I am most familiar with it in the university context, where the lines are usually drawn between those who favor combining composition with some university subject like literature and those who regard all extrinsic subject matter, however valuable in itself, as irrelevant to the teaching of writing skills.

The earlier discussions of this book carry some implications for curricular decisions of this sort, and these implications should be brought into the light. Everything I have learned from my researches points toward the correctness of the second point of view—that composition is a craft which cannot properly be subsumed under any conventional subject matter. It is not a branch of literary study, or logic, or even of rhetoric. Even in composition courses, there are good reasons for giving instruction in those three fields. But to stress such instruction is a very inefficient way of teaching composition.

In talking with many university teachers of composition, I have become convinced that one reason for the desire to mix composition with other instructional goals is the ignorance that besets us all about effective ways to teach composition. We know a lot more about literature than we know about teaching the craft of prose. In our anxious ignorance on that subject, we commit ourselves to goals that are more "humanistic" than mere composition. Yet the humanists of the Renaissance thought that a good prose style was a chief goal of culture, and a sound case can be made for their view. [1] Literature and logic are worthy subjects of study. But these subjects *are* offered in the universities; they do not need to be presented in large doses to a captive audience in a required course whose announced goal is the teaching of writing. Let me review some of the considerations that have brought me to this opinion.

First, it can be shown that knowing how to write is different from knowing about literature. The proof is simple. Numbers of graduate students in literature are unable to write well, yet they do demonstrably know a great deal about literature, much more than a freshman could possibly learn in a composition course. Whatever the theory may have been under which the teaching of literature was thought to be closely connected with writing skills, that theory has been shown to be incorrect by this simple empirical test.

There is, moreover, a strong reason for separating the teaching of writing from the teaching of literature. While both subjects may make students aware of style, they do so in conflicting ways. The study of style in literature is a study of the *fusion* of form with content. But learning how to write implies just the opposite assumption; it assumes the *separation* of linguistic form and content. Learning the craft of prose is learning to write the *same* meaning in a different and more effective way. This conflict of assumptions between literary study and composition teaching was accurately described by Milic some years ago, and his cogent argument has never been refuted. [2]

The case for making logic the governing subject is hardly better. The vogue of introducing formal logic into the composition classroom has now passed, but chapters on logical fallacies still appear in the composition handbooks—a concession to the inextinguishable belief that "clear" writing and "clear" thinking reflect each other. The belief is venerable. But everyone will surely want to keep the belief from impairing effective instruction in

1. J. Huizinga, *Men and Ideas*, trans. J. S. Holmes and H. van Marle (New York, 1959), p. 245.
2. L. T. Milic, "Theories of Style and Their Implications for the Teaching of Composition," *College Composition and Communication* 16 (1965): 2–6.

composition. Highly logical and clear-headed students often write badly because they fail to make explicit some of the implicit logical connections in their argument. But even when they make such connections, they may still write badly. There is, in fact, a logical flaw in equating clear thinking and clear writing. The word *clear* means something different in the two phrases. Clear thinking means drawing correct inferences from the given premises. Clear writing means an unambiguous and readable expression of one's meaning. I have argued, and have illustrated the point, that muddy writing can express clear thinking and that clear writing can express muddy thinking. [3]

Often, when I have stated this kind of opinion in conversation with my colleagues, I have stirred up misgivings. I must therefore assume that some of my readers will also be troubled by my separatist views. I wish therefore to concede the point that there is often a connection between quality of writing and of thought, whether or not it is a necessary connection. My concern in raising the issue is a practical one. I believe, as a practical matter, that instruction in logic is a very inefficient way to give instruction in writing. It is largely, I think, a waste of valuable time. So long as fallacy-lists and truth tables are left outside the writing class, it does not matter—except perhaps in grading policy—whether the teacher is a separatist. Moreover, the practical question of whether logic instruction is an efficient way to teach "clear" writing is a question that could be definitively answered. One good piece of empirical research would yield the answer.

Similar practical and theoretical difficulties beset the attempt to make composition a branch of rhetoric. I should say right away in favor of the attempt that it is sounder than subsuming composition under logic or literature. For rhetoric is at least a practical art, like writing. And there is a strong rhetorical element in writing, since an author is normally concerned with the effect of his text on a reader and must, like the rhetorician, take account of his audience. One can even say, on those grounds, that there is a strong rhetorical element in most speech, whether oral or written.

But on that line of reasoning one could argue—and some have argued—that linguistics should be the subsuming discipline for composition. Linguistics really does cover all domains of speech. But that is part of the trouble with rhetoric and linguistics. They are not coextensive with composition. Many of their concerns are as irrelevant to composition as the concerns of literature and logic.

3. See p. 87 above.

No sensible writing teacher will make his students learn the terms, concepts, and history of rhetoric, and there is a lot of evidence to suggest that sensible writing teachers have recently abandoned instruction in the concepts and terms of linguistics.

Rhetoric, then, is the subject closest to composition, both because the concerns of the two subjects overlap in many places and because they are both practical arts. All the more reason, therefore, to warn against a premature subsumption of composition under rhetoric. The nearness of the fit makes the subsumption of composition under rhetoric all the more misleading. A legal statute may be well or badly written, while remaining indifferent to its emotive or persuasive effects on readers. The same is true of many instructional manuals and even many technical articles. That does not put these genres beyond the pale. They are highly important kinds of writing, and it is highly important that they should be well-written.

The attempts to subsume composition under conventional university subjects like logic, literature, linguistics, and rhetoric, have in common the hidden assumption that composition must come under *some* humanistic subject matter. Certainly it is true that a number of different subject matters have a bearing on the pedagogy and theory of composition. But to subsume composition itself under a traditional subject is like subsuming the practical art of drawing under the history of art. To learn how to write is to gain practical, not theoretical, knowledge. Writing needs to be taught as a practical, not a theoretical, subject. The teacher of drawing asks his students to make drawings, and then comments on what his students have produced. That is the basic character of teaching in all the practical arts, including the art of writing. The teaching can be done well or badly, and teachers can learn how to do it well.

The place of composition among other school and university subjects is its own place. It is not part of another subject matter but a branch of practical knowledge in its own right. In relation to our culture as a whole, it is a kind of knowledge that has an importance equal to any other subject in the curriculum, except reading. And if it is reasonable to assume that almost every college student can read, then it follows that composition is a subject of unrivaled importance at the university. When Erasmus spoke of the great cultural renaissance of his time as a revival of *bonae litterae*, he meant a revival of what we would now call composition. [4]

4. Huizinga, *Men and Ideas*, p. 245.

Some Typical Rules and Maxims

Herbert Spencer's attempt to reduce all stylistic maxims to a single principle was in fact a successful attempt. But the practical difficulty with Spencer's principle of economy is its generality. He conceded that the long way round can be the most economical way for many a particular semantic intention; thus, *magnificent* can be better than *grand*, and a long, complex sentence can be better than a short, simple one. His universal imperative is simply that we should choose the most economical expression from among those different expressions which serve the same purpose. But his principle does not tell us how to judge either psychological economy or sameness of purpose in particular cases. Spencer simplified the problem of style by abstracting it, but then omitted to give the student practical help in making concrete decisions.

But "practical" maxims have their own problems. If they are many they can confuse the student, and if they are few they can mislead him. Probably no single maxim of composition holds for all cases. If a student is told "use concrete rather than abstract words," that maxim will fail him in a good many instances. And if the student is also instructed to "use appropriate words," the two maxims will sometimes be in conflict. No doubt, practical maxims are highly useful to students of writing and will always be needed, but they cannot always be applied with confidence. They suffer some of the same difficulties as Spencer's general principle, in that the student cannot be sure of their proper application in particular cases. The proper application of both a maxim and a principle requires a difficult practical judgment. Because of this exigency, a general principle (being always true) is often more practical than a directly practical maxim. To place confidence in maxims alone is to lean on a weak reed.

But experience suggests that maxims are indispensable devices in teaching any practical art. If our aim is to teach writing more efficiently, then we may find it useful to distinguish the more important maxims from the less important ones. It would be useful to know, for instance, which set of maxims will normally help the student achieve basic writing proficiency in the shortest time. This information is not now known, though research could probably yield it. What I propose to do in this and the following section is to make some guesses about the relative utility of maxims in composition pedagogy.

But here I must enter a caveat. The experienced teacher of

composition will have nothing to learn from my comments on practical pedagogy and may wonder why I have not even mentioned such well-tested techniques as sentence-combining and peer-group teaching. Such a reader should simply move directly to the last section of this chapter. For him, what I shall go on to discuss up to that point will seem far less important than the previous, theoretical parts of the book. But I include these practical observations because some of my readers will find them useful, and others will perceive their wider, theoretical implications. For instance, it is important for me to show, in documenting my theoretical case, that the tried and true maxims of composition turn out to correlate very well with the psychological principles of readability. No maxim, of course, will be always important for all ages and all students. One that has little generality, such as "Make a series consistent and climactic" (Crews), may be of great importance for a student who often writes a series. [5] No rating of maxims can be altogether reliable, since different students will have different deficiencies—a consideration which points again to the superior utility of general principles over practical maxims. But, despite these variables, I believe it will be illuminating to analyze some of the accumulated practical wisdom of the handbooks in the light of the preceding chapters of this book.

To do this, I shall excerpt some typical imperatives from five representative handbooks: Strunk, Gowers, McCrimmon, Crews, and Lucas. [6] Following the patterns set by Strunk, I shall phrase all the maxims as imperatives, though, in many current handbooks (for instance in McCrimmon), these imperatives are presented as declarative statements or as questions.

Strunk
1. Choose a suitable design and hold to it.
2. Make the paragraph the unit of composition.
3. Use the active voice.
4. Put statements in positive form.
5. Use definite, specific, concrete language.
6. Omit needless words.
7. Avoid a succession of loose sentences.

5. F. Crews, *The Random House Handbook* (New York, 1974).
6. E. Gowers, *The Complete Plain Words* (London, 1954); F. L. Lucas, *Style* (New York, 1955); J. M. McCrimmon, *Writing with a Purpose* (Boston, 1975); W. Strunk and E. B. White, *The Elements of Style* (New York, 1959).

8. Express co-ordinate ideas in similar form.
9. Keep related words together.
10. In summaries, keep to one tense.
11. Place the emphatic words of a sentence at the end.

Gowers
1. Know what you want to say.
2. Use appropriate words.
3. Think for others rather than for yourself.
4. Be simple and short.
5. Be human but correct.
6. Don't vainly resist new words.
7. Avoid padding.
8. Choose the familiar word.
9. Keep related words together.
10. Avoid ambiguous word order and phrasing.

McCrimmon
1. Choose and restrict your subject.
2. Make and test an outline.
3. Write unified and complete paragraphs.
4. Make them follow a definite order.
5. Use transitional devices in paragraphs: i.e., pronouns, repetition, parallel forms.
6. Use concrete detail.
7. Vary sentence types.
8. Use appropriate words.
9. Use concrete words.
10. Keep an appropriate tone and style throughout.

Crews
1. Keep to your point.
2. Use an appropriate and consistent tone.
3. Use appropriate words.
4. Avoid clichés, jargon, and circumlocution.
5. Use vivid and lively language.
6. Vary sentence structure and length.
7. Make unified paragraphs.
8. Make good transitions between paragraphs.
9. Use coordination.
10. Make a series consistent and climactic.
11. Link sentences together.
12. Make the first and last paragraph count.

Lucas
1. Make your own character seem good.
2. Make clear connections between sentences.
3. Don't say too many things at once.
4. Don't get lured off the line of argument.
5. Use short paragraphs rather than long.
6. Avoid monotony.
7. Be simple.
8. Omit needless words.
9. Write less; rewrite more.
10. Variety is courtesy to the reader.

The similarities among these lists will inspire a certain amount of confidence. The handbooks are still saying what they said in Herbert Spencer's day and before: use familiar, concrete words; keep related words together; and so on. A number of the injunctions listed above are saying very similar things in different ways. For instance, where Strunk says "Choose a suitable design and stick to it," we find in Crews "Keep to your point," in McCrimmon "choose and restrict your subject," and in Gowers "Know what you want to say." We could even draw up a list of equivalences for some of these injunctions (see fig. 1).

Anyone looking at figure 1 will be struck by the relatively bad fit of Gowers with the rest of the group. The reason for this will illuminate the nature of composition maxims in general. Gowers's excellent handbook, though widely used in Britain by teachers and journalists, was originally addressed to government bureaucrats. It was issued as an official government white paper whose purpose was to improve the style of official reports and letters to members of the public. Gowers assumed that the bureaucrat he addressed knew how to spell, punctuate, and form paragraphs. Since his book was aimed at the characteristic failings of bureaucratic writing, he chose not to discuss coordination, transitions, or even sentence variety. Most of his civil-servant audience had mastered those elements of style. What they had failed to master was brevity, humanity, simplicity, and clarity. That is where Gowers bore down hard and effectively. He wanted official letters to be less pompous and confusing, to say what they had to say, and to project a common humanity rather than the writer's arcane superiority. Since his audience was different from the audience for college handbooks, so were his composition maxims different from those addressed to freshmen.

Fig. 1. Stylistic maxims from handbooks.

	Strunk	Gowers
1	Choose a suitable design and stick to it.	Know what you want to say.
2	Use definite, specific, concrete language.	Choose the concrete and familiar word.
3	Omit needless words.	Avoid padding and jargon.
4	Make the paragraph the unit of composition.	
5	Avoid a succession of loose sentences.	
6	Express coordinate ideas in similar form.	
7		Avoid ambiguous word order.
8		Use appropriate words.
9	Keep related words together.	Keep related words together.

This contrast leads directly to an inference about the relative importance of different stylistic maxims. You cannot list them in the order of their importance unless you take into account the learners to whom the maxims are addressed, and unless you also consider the chief kinds of writing which those learners are undertaking to learn. If your learners are not going to announce official rulings in letters and reports to a helpless public, then Gowers's maxim "Be human," will be lower on your list than "Write unified paragraphs."

But if it is true that the pedagogical value of a maxim will vary with the audience and the genre of writing, then it must follow that no single list of maxims will serve all purposes. And that is another way of saying that we cannot depend upon maxims alone in the teaching of composition. We need to teach genuine *principles* of composition as well—the principles behind the maxims. That is what every good writer has learned, with or without the aid of the handbooks.

Does this mean, as a practical matter, that students should be given different sets of maxims for different genres—a set for college

McCrimmon	Crews	Lucas
Choose and restrict your subject.	Keep to your point.	Don't get lured off your line of argument.
Use concrete details and words.	Use vivid and lively language.	Be simple and concrete.
Avoid jargon.	Avoid clichés, jargon, and circumlocution.	Omit needless words.
Write in unified and complete paragraphs.	Write in unified and coherent paragraphs.	Write in short paragraphs.
Vary sentence types.	Vary sentence structure and length.	Variety of sentences is a courtesy to the reader.
Use transitional devices such as parallel forms.	Use coordination to link sentences together.	Make clear the connection between sentences.
Revise for clarity and emphasis.		Don't say too many things at once.
Use appropriate words.	Use appropriate words.	

essays, a set for personal letters, a set for stories, a set for newspaper articles? This might be an effective method if the various kinds of writing were very different in their requirements. But, in fact, every genre of prose exhibits much variety, and also a lot of overlap with other genres. A good college essay may contain narrative elements; it may exploit some of the informalities of a letter, and also some of the reporting methods of a newspaper article. Or it may take the form of a technical scientific report. No genre, not even the technical, scientific article, has watertight conventions. In my experience, a student who can write well in one genre can quickly learn to write well in another. He possesses a general proficiency that is transferable to many different genres. That is what one would expect if the principles *behind* the maxims were general principles, applicable to all genres of prose.

Does this mean that writing would be taught more efficiently if we dispensed with maxims altogether and taught principles instead? Common sense replies "No." The principles are too abstract. But it might be the case that writing would be taught more efficiently if the *teachers* knew the principles behind the maxims. Armed with that knowledge, the teacher (or the self-teacher) could decide which maxims were the most important ones for a particular student at a particular time.

The Relation of Maxims to Psychological Principles

Among the five handbooks from which I have extracted writing maxims, only the one by Strunk gives prominence to the rule "Put statements in positive form." The other four writers probably considered this rule vulnerable to too many exceptions. Yet every concrete rule of style is open to exceptions, even the rule "Omit needless words." When is a word needless? Translated into concrete instructions, the rule says something like this: "Be brief, and when in doubt about the functional importance of a word omit it." Yet, so stated, this rule is open to many exceptions. Inexperienced writers are often too brief. They supply too little explicit context, and thereby unintentionally leave the reader with too many uncertainties. In giving a precise rule about positive statements, Strunk did at least give students a rule they could directly use. But any directly usable stylistic rule is open to exceptions. The accurate form of all such maxims is: "Do X, unless you have weighty reasons for not doing X." The point in giving the rule is that doing X will be better than not doing X—most of the time.

If that is the nature of all stylistic maxims, then Strunk's rule about positive statements must count as an excellent one. In most cases, positive statements will be more readable than negative ones. Strunk knew by experience what psycholinguists have now established by experiment, namely, that we understand positive statements more rapidly than negative ones, because positives are psychologically more linear than negatives.[7] With a negative we normally first understand its positive sense, and then we take the second step of negating this positive sense. Hence in most verbal contexts, "the book is shut" is easier than "the book is not open." Yet we cannot dispense with negative statements. If we could, negatives probably would have tended to drop out of speech.

The same pattern holds for the maxim shared by all five authors: "Use concrete language." There is good evidence from

---

7. T. Trabasso, H. Rollins, and E. Shaughnessy, "Storage and Verification in Processing Concepts," *Cognitive Psychology* 2 (1971): 239–89.

recent experiments that we do take up meaning more securely from concrete than from abstract words.[8] It is usually better to say "The pen is mightier than the sword" than to say "Writing is more effective than warfare." Similarly, we can understand familiar words more rapidly than rare ones, thus justifying Gowers's rule: "Use the familiar word." But these stylistic rules are not reliable; they are only rules of thumb. For some purposes, abstract words are better than concrete words, and rare words better than familiar ones. Stylistic rules always imply an unless clause: "Use the familiar word, *unless* the rare one suits your purpose better." Use the concrete word, *unless* the abstract one works better." What the student needs to know, and what every practiced writer does know, is that he usually sacrifices some degree of readability when he breaks the rule. The sacrifice is worthwhile if it serves accurate communication.

The stylistic rules just mentioned are all concerned with making clauses easier to process. Other rules which enhance the readability of clauses are: "Use the active voice," "Keep related words together," and "Avoid ambiguous word order." And indeed, the active voice *is* usually easier to process than the passive. To keep related words together *does* effect more rapid semantic closure than to separate them. And using an unambiguous word order *does* cut down processing time for the reader. The maxims are therefore quite sound variations on the general principle that the writer ought to enhance the readability of his clauses so long as that stylistic aim is consonant with his semantic purposes.

The other maxims, by and large, concern the readability of units larger than the clause. And these maxims tend to be more general in application than the clause rules. The injunction to vary sentence structure must come as close to universality as any maxim of writing. Being boring is hard to defend on any grounds. I can think of only one defense of it—that the writer *wants* to be boring.

There is also a sound psychological reason for stressing the paragraph as the unit of composition, no matter what the genre of prose might be. The universality of the rule arises from the universality of the attention mechanism. One-thing-at-a-time is

8. M. K. Johnson, J. D. Bransford, S. E. Nyberg, J. J. Cleary, "Comprehension Factors in Interpreting Memory for Abstract and Concrete Sentences," *Journal of Verbal Learning and Verbal Behavior* 8 (1972): 451–54.

its governing principle, and its corollary in writing is one-theme-at-a-time. Since the mind works sequentially, nothing is gained by taking up a second theme before the first one has been understood. This principle of closure works on the large scale of the text as well as the small scale of the clause. A theme must have some degree of semantic closure before it can function as a textual element in long-term memory. If the paragraph did not exist, we would have to invent it. It is to a text as a clause is to a sentence and a phrase is to a clause.

Equally general is the principle of choosing a design and sticking to it. This is a readability rule that is closely connected with the typical differences between oral and written speech. It is a rule that has to be taught, precisely because it is not a general need in oral speech. Recorded oral discourse is punctuated with false starts, changes of mind, changes of subject in the middle of sentences. When transcribed, such discourse approaches unintelligibility. In written discourse, you have to choose a design and stick to it, because the discourse itself is the chief context of the utterance. To change the design is to change the context and therefore to throw into uncertainty what the reader thought he was understanding. Some writers use such shifts deliberately, but in so doing they do not thereby break the rule. In order for a reader to grasp that his confusion is an intended effect, he must assume that it was part of the original design.

Finally, the other large-scale rules of coherence are also firmly grounded in the psychology of readability. The use of parallel forms to present similar ideas will speed up understanding by exploiting the principle of short-term expectancy.[9] We expect a subsequent event to resemble closely a preceding event, especially when the two have common features. When we read writing that has followed this rule of parallel form, our first meaning-hypothesis will tend to be the right one, and this is a crucial feature of readable prose.

Other expectation-fulfilling rules have an importance which many handbooks fail to stress sufficiently. Where the handbooks emphasize large-scale organization and the writing of outlines, they might better stress shorter-term devices of semantic integration. Although an implicit plan is essential, explicit integration-techniques have an even wider range of application than the making of explicit written outlines. While written outlines are

9. See p. 102–3 above.

highly useful for the expository essays required in college courses, they are not absolutely essential devices for choosing a design and sticking to it. On the other hand, good prose cannot dispense with short-term devices of expectation-fulfillment between phrases, clauses, sentences, and paragraphs.

One such integrative device, far more essential to writing than to oral speech, is the proleptic word or phrase: *but, similarly, also, on the other hand, moreover, by contrast, nonetheless, likewise, therefore, however,* and so on. These devices deserve to have a high-ranking maxim all to themselves: "Use proleptic words or phrases unless the relation between elements is quickly obvious without using them." The rule is important because proleptic devices serve the double function of constraining the meaning of the ongoing clause and integrating that meaning with earlier ones. Proleptics thereby speed up understanding and integrate meaning, despite the absence of intonation- and situation-clues which perform these two functions in oral speech.

Another integrative device of equal importance and universality is the thematic tag. A tag word or phrase in a preceding clause should be repeated in the one that follows. Although variety demands that such repetitions be sometimes effected by pronouns or synonymous words and phrases, the principle of repetition is unavoidable in good writing. The tags need not always be repeated relentlessly through the whole discourse, since particular lexical and syntactic forms are normally forgotten rather quickly after a few intervening sentences. The repeated tags serve their principal function across closely adjoining sentences, where they can integrate a sequence of meanings before lexical memory has begun to decay.

The two maxims I have just stressed—*Use proleptic devices* and *Use thematic tags*—are not usually given appropriate prominence in the handbooks. Their relative neglect can probably be traced back to the lack of coordinated research into composition. Only recently have psychological researchers discovered the previously unsuspected fact that we rapidly forget linguistic forms. Without knowledge of that fact, it was easy for handbook writers to underestimate the importance of short-term integrative devices between adjoining sentences. These middle-range devices seemed less important than either large-scale thematic organization or small-scale stylistic choices within clauses. But, in fact, the integrative, middle-range techniques of writing are probably the most important techniques to be taught. They bridge the gap between readable single sentences and readable discourse. Because such integrative techniques are often unnecessary in a student's ordinary oral speech, it is a good bet that further research will show the middle-range maxims to have a very great pedagogical importance.

In these two brief sections on typical maxims of composition, I have tried to show, among other things, that practical experience in the classroom coincides pretty well with the psychological principles of readability. The discussion has shown that Herbert Spencer's insight was a sound one, and that psychological economy *is* the governing principle which determines the most effective written expression of one's intended meaning. Each of the practical maxims of composition was shown to enhance "the economy of the reader's attention," just as Spencer had predicted.

But some of the typical rules appeared to be more important than others, and also to be more general in their application. In achieving "economy of attention" at the level of clause and phrase, the most important rules seem to be:

1. *Omit needless words.*
2. *Keep related words together.*

These two rules assure rapid semantic closure when the reader is processing a clause. If the writer omits extensive qualifications between a noun and verb, for instance, the reader can quickly achieve semantic closure without taxing his short-term memory. The same economy of the reader's attention is achieved when the writer keeps related words together, and for the same reason. Omitting intervening phrases will ease the reader's job in the same way as omitting intervening words. Both techniques reduce the burden that is placed on the reader's short-term memory.

Here is an example taken quite at random:

> Once again the data force the conclusion that trigram frequency, as measured by counting the frequency of three-letter sequences in printed text, does not predict learning when those trigrams are responses in paired-associate lists.

This can be revised on the basis of our two maxims even by someone who lacks a precise knowledge of the subject matter:

> Once again the data will show that trigram frequency does not predict learning. Trigram frequency is measured by counting the frequency of three-letter sequences in printed text. When we examine these same trigrams as responses in paired-

associate lists, we find that their frequency does not predict
how well they will be learned.

The gain in readability comes only indirectly from converting one
long sentence into three short ones. Sentence length is at best an
indirect indication of readability. My main reasons for breaking
up the long sentence were to keep related words together and to
omit needless intervening words.

If we turn from these two rules which mainly ease the burden
on short-term memory, we will find that the most important
remaining rules are those which channel the reader's attention,
constrain his meaning-guesses, and integrate his understanding.
Most of the typical maxims perform several of these functions at
once, which is not surprising if we notice the close connection
between the functions themselves. When the reader's attention is
channeled, his meaning-guesses will also be constrained, and his
understood meanings will therefore tend to be integrated with
one another. On this reasoning, the most important remaining
rules would be those which serve to channel the reader's attention.

If I had to choose just two more maxims of writing, I would try
to find two which channeled the reader's attention over an
extended stretch of discourse and which thereby forced the writer
unconsciously to obey several readability maxims at once. My
choices would be:

3. *Make the paragraph the unit of composition.*
4. *Use integrative devices between clauses and sentences.*

The first maxim would constrain the reader's semantic expectations on the large scale, and therefore economize his efforts to
understand the gist of the text. The second maxim would constrain
and economize the reader's effort in the middle range between his
clause processing and his overall understanding.

The admonition to write in paragraphs implies that the theme of
the paragraph be set early, even if not in the form of a summary
topic sentence. The reader cannot understand the meaning of a
clause sequence until he understands its main theme. This theme
has to be expressed by verbal means, since it cannot be found in a
concrete, nonverbal situation. To write in paragraphs therefore
implies an explicit focus on a theme for a long enough time to
contextualize and constrain the clauses which convey the writer's
meaning. Paragraphs do not always "develop an idea." But they
do serve in principle to contextualize a theme long enough and

explicitly enough to constrain the reader's meaning-expectations on the larger scale.

The smaller-scale devices that serve to unify a paragraph do so by integrating its sequence of clauses and sentences. The key element in all such integration devices is the element of adjacent repetition. To use parallel forms in adjacent phrases and clauses is to repeat a form and therefore fulfill an expectation. (But it is pointless to repeat a syntactic form from a distant sentence, since the reader will not dependably remember the earlier form.) Even the use of proleptic words like *however*, is a kind of adjacent repetition, since the qualification predicted by the *however* requires a remembering and therefore an implicit repetition of the adjacent meaning that is being qualified. Similarly, the use of thematic tags will require repetition between neighboring clauses, either by duplicating the words or representing them by pronouns and synonyms.

The conscious use of these adjacent repetitions serves both to integrate clause sequences and also to vary their character and length. Repetition indirectly combats monotony. For, paradoxically, the use of integrative repetitions in nearby phrases will force variations on the writer by compelling him to rearrange his word sequences. In trying to achieve some form of repetition before the reader forgets the earlier element, the writer will often need to depart from the more usual syntactical arrangement. The following three sentences by Sapir illustrate how the need for adjacent repetitions will induce variations in syntax and sentence length:

> Probably the most important single source of changes in vocabulary is the creation of new words on analogies which have spread from a few specific words.
>
> Of the linguistic changes due to the more obvious types of contact, the one which seems to have played the most important part in the history of languages is the "borrowing" of words across linguistic frontiers. This borrowing goes hand in hand with cultural diffusion.

The main pattern of repetition here is *changes—changes* and *borrowing—borrowing*. In order to achieve this integrative repetition, Sapir began his new paragraph with an *of* clause that varys from ordinary syntax. An eye to such integrative repetitions will induce similar syntactic variations in every writer. And if the writer also keeps explicit the main theme of his paragraph, the repetition of thematic tags will serve both to integrate his clauses and unify his paragraph as a whole.

In choosing these four maxims for their generality and power, I am not suggesting that they will prove to be the most efficient maxims for teaching composition. They might turn out to be so; they are at least few in number, and therefore easily managed by the student. But so many factors are at work in the composing process, and also in the learning process, that any present prediction about the efficient use of maxims is just a stab in the dark. Reliable evaluation of such predictions will have to await reliable research.

Improving Teaching Methods

What are the main practical implications of the foregoing pages for teaching composition to real students in real situations? I cannot pretend to tell the talented and experienced teacher anything he doesn't already know. But, for my less experienced readers, not to confront this question at all would be an evasion as great as replying to it merely with hopeful predictions about further research. On teaching methods we already have a mountain of research, but those who dig there return empty-handed and discouraged. The mountain contains, to put the matter bluntly, mostly inferior ore. The research is often conducted by persons untrained in the design and interpretation of psychosocial experiments; the variables are rarely kept under control; the statistical inferences are rarely sophisticated. Worst of all, the judgment of writing quality is left either to impressionism or to a mechanical counting system. We cannot expect good research in teaching methods until we develop sound ways to evaluate writing quality. Since we have to judge a teaching method by its results, and since we have developed no reliable method for gauging results, we cannot reasonably expect to find hidden treasure in the existing mountain of research on composition. I hope that in the future the criterion of relative readability will be accepted as the qualitative standard for well-grounded research into the effectiveness of teaching methods.

But even greatly improved research will leave unanswered some important questions about teaching. The personality of the student and of the instructor will be crucial factors not covered in the statistics. The teacher will always need to emphasize different maxims with different students. In training the author of the following passage, the teacher would hardly want to stress the maxim "Use proleptic devices."

My Opinion of the Anthony Burgess Essay "Is America Falling Apart?"

The argument that Mr. Burgess has formulated is not very organized. First of all, he begins his essay by criticizing America. Following this criticism, he concedes that some good things do exist in the United States, and he proceeds to discuss them. Then, he changes his argument around by listing more of the ugly aspects of American life. However, Burgess concludes the essay by once again praising America. Furthermore, many of his sentences are ambiguous. An example of this ambiguity is found in the following sentence: "This is what the human condition is about." It is not clear to the reader exactly what the "this" in the preceding sentence is referring to. Also, quite frequently Burgess separates the subject from the predicate. "The nightmare of filth, outside and in, that unfolds on the trip from Springfield, Mass., to Grand Central Station, would not be accepted in backward Europe." There are too many words between the subject and the predicate of this sentence.

The comments which the teacher did in fact write down on this passage were not very helpful. The student was advised to convert "is referring to" into "refers to" because the present indicative is all that is needed. The student's *ambiguous—ambiguity* was found to be "repetitive," and so on. While the teacher quite properly withheld ironic remarks about the content of the passage, he said little that the student could use to improve a similar passage in the future.

Both this passage and the comments on it are highly typical. A C-level composition student is often doing a better job than his teacher in performing his appointed task. For the student usually has a clearer idea about his semantic intentions in his paper than the teacher has about his pedagogical purposes in making comments on it. We need maxims for paper-*marking* fully as much as we need maxims for paper-writing. While the differentness of students will always require the use of the teacher's judgment, we can hope that, despite student differences, research can discover the most frequently effective methods for marking papers.

Meanwhile, in the absence of such research, it is possible to make some informed guesses about the best ways to write comments on student papers. This attempt is worth making, for very probably written comments will turn out to be the most effective teaching device of all. Let me explain this guess before I suggest some actual maxims for comment writing.

To teach any practical art, a teacher always builds on the practical knowledge that his student already has. In teaching tennis, the coach first tells the beginner to grip the racket by "shaking hands," since presumably he already knows how to shake hands. If the student has played baseball, his backhand will be "like batting left-handed," and his serve will be "like throwing an overarm pitch." The coach will then make corrective changes in the motions that the student actually produces. The basis for this kind of instruction is the principle of the *schema*, to use Piaget's term. A person learns something new by building on a schema already known, and in practical knowledge the already known form is a productive "schema" for performing a task. Gombrich has suggested that illusionist painters followed a development based on gradual changes in the existing schemata for representing the world.[10] I have conjectured in Chapter 3 that the history of prose followed a similar development, one which individual students must to some extent repeat. To make comments on a student's paper is to build upon productive schemata which the student already has, and to encourage their expansion and improvement. Because the comment method is so direct and so widespread in all forms of practical instruction, we can reasonably assume that it has the highest importance in composition teaching.

Well-conceived commenting on papers, then, is probably more effective than formal lectures on composition or even Socratic questions about composition. There is a place for such methods, of course, but pure lecturing is probably the least efficient method of teaching any practical art. The most efficient method will probably turn out to be direct written commentary on the student's performance, coupled with ad hoc discussions of the problems that have often cropped up in a particular group. The great advantages of the written commentary are its individuality and permanence. The student can study the comment several times and in principle can learn something permanent from it.

10. E. H. Gombrich, *Art and Illusion* (New York, 1960).

I list the following maxims of commentary with some diffidence. Only the importance of the subject impels me to take a stand on matters about which we must all feel rather uncertain in the absence of good research.

1. *Comment on just two or three points in any paper.*

If the comments are to effect an improvement, they must be taken to heart and kept in mind by the student. And if the student is to keep the comments in mind when he writes again, they must be few in number, because his capacities are already heavily taxed by the act of writing. He cannot think of ten new points all at once. The worst vice of the schoolmarm is to correct everything. Of course, in some cases, it might be effective to correct more faults than one comments upon.

2. *Select those matters for comment which are most important for an individual student at a particular time.*

The chief talent of the teacher resides in the diagnostic ability that enables him to make this kind of selection. In the passage on Burgess, just quoted, the main fault demanding commentary was the deficiency of the stated theme in integrating the sentences of the paragraph. Instead of the topic, "not very organized," the student needed a theme like "ambiguous" and needed to repeat this word as an explicit leitmotif. A second criticism, admonishing the student to vary sentence form and length, would have sufficed as commentary.

3. *Summarize the commentary in a usable form.*

Since the point of commentary is future, not past, performance, it should be put in a form that makes it available for future use by the student. The most useful form is probably a short paragraph referring to particular examples of a general point. Students and teachers will do well to conquer the assumption that the red ink on a paper is the defense of a grade. Most of the red ink ought to be in the summary.

4. *Begin writing comments only after a rapid analysis of the paper as a whole.*

This will save time and ink and will make the remarks more pointed and effective.

5. *Choose those comments which will be likely to induce the greatest improvement in the intrinsic effectiveness of the student's next paper.*

This spells out the principle for following maxim 2, namely, select only the most important matters for comment.

6. *State the comments in an encouraging manner.*

While a scolding tone may be just what is needed on occasion, the best results are likely to be produced by encouragement. Since this seems to be true in all the crafts, it is probably true in composition. It is also true that occasional expressions of dissatisfaction are also effective since they mean that one expects serious efforts.

7. *Do not hesitate to repeat a comment over several papers.*

If the teacher's analysis is accurate, repetition of a comment is going to be an effective teaching device. A lot of rehearsal is needed to change a student's productive schemata.

8. *Keep track of the comments, so that nothing of great importance for a particular student is omitted during the course.*

The teacher can accomplish this by keeping an abbreviated record in his gradebook. This record is useful also for student conferences. Obviously, the student should keep his own papers and should be instructed to review the comments on them.

9. *Make clear from the tone of the comments that they deal with a craft to be learned and not with the teacher's personal taste.*

Students of the subject usually believe that they are catering to their teacher's whims. E. B. White thought and apparently still thinks that his teacher, Strunk, was expressing his own definite and forthright personality when he ordered his students to put statements in a positive form. Students, on their side, believe that tampering with their styles is tampering with their personalities. This makes the whole subject seem a serious invasion of privacy. That is a tangled half-truth which the teacher needs to untangle for his students and himself.

After comments, the most important device for teaching effective writing is probably directed revision. Of course, the principles for directing a revision will reside ultimately within the student himself. To put them there is the goal of teaching—the goal of the teacher's comments. Any writer's first draft is already the product of a revision process in which some forms have been rejected in favor of others on the basis of editorial principles which the writer has internalized. But even a practiced writer will need to make further revisions in his first draft if he has directed a lot of his attention to the substance rather than the form of his discourse. But whether the editing/revising process occurs chiefly in the first draft or in a later one, revision principles are still central to the writer's craft. To learn writing is to learn principles of revision.

It follows from this that teaching methods will be effective to the extent that they teach students how to revise their prose to make it readable. The most efficient way of teaching revision principles will probably turn out to be the most efficient way of teaching composition. Here, again, it is reasonable to suppose that research will show the direct approach to be the most efficient teaching method, and that a large proportion of teaching time should be directly concerned with revising what has already been written. The energy that a student expends in composing a first draft is diffused in several directions, all of them undoubtedly instructive but not always efficient in improving his ability to produce effective prose. Contrariwise, the energy he expends in applying revision principles is very directly aimed at learning those principles and improving his productive schemata as a writer.

The practical inferences to be drawn from these considerations are not clear-cut. So many factors are involved in writing and in composition teaching that it would be foolish to recommend a simple formula for allotting the time spent on actual revisions. My own experience as a composition teacher leads me to believe that it is a good technique to make about every third assignment a revision assignment based on the teacher's earlier comments. I also have found that to spend class time in publicly revising a text is an efficient teaching method. So is the method of using class time for individual writing and revising. When the composition class is thus conceived as a workshop, the students perceive its utility to themselves and tend, in my experience, to be highly motivated. They understand what they are doing and observe their own progress.

Another revision method that I have found to be successful is one that has only recently been given a sanction in psychological research. In order to demonstrate the genuine utility of revising to achieve readable prose, I have read aloud from student papers and then tested the group's understanding of what was read. The advantage of this oral method over visual presentation is that the listener is unable to circle back and reprocess an earlier section of the text. Hence, the linearity of the prose can be rather accurately gauged by such a comprehension test. This method has been validated by recent research which shows that the readability of a text is the same as its listenability.[11]

11. I. E. Fang, "The Easy Listening Formula," *Journal of Broadcasting* 11

Another method that seems highly promising is to isolate the teaching of composition from the giving of final grades. The pedagogical advantage of the method is the obvious one that teacher and student become colleagues in a joint enterprise, rather than suspicious adversaries. The entire aim of the enterprise is to produce good writers, as determined by an outside test, and so everyone's energies are directed to that aim. This scheme can work only if reliable outside tests are developed. But unless reliable tests of writing proficiency are indeed developed, we cannot make serious progress in either teaching or research; nor can we make objective evaluations of either students or teachers of composition.

The use of these three techniques—effective written commentary, revision-practice in and out of class, and third-party evaluation of final results—will probably make the teaching of writing more efficient than it normally is. But the best way to apply these techniques is unknown, and their applicability to different age-levels is untested. My own practical experience has been gained in teaching and directing college-level courses, where the main craft to be taught is how to compose readable rather than "correct," normalized prose. Yet readability does depend on the normalization of spelling, grammar, punctuation, and word usage. Correctness in these four sorts of convention is therefore a matter of some importance, and any college-level student who is seriously deficient in them will need additional training.

But two of these four primary conventions involve a competence very different from that required for the other two and deserve very different kinds of attention by the teacher. Spelling and punctuation are purely scribal conventions, which need to be learned from the start by all native speakers. They are basic tools that require memorization, like the multiplication table and, like it, are best learned early. But grammar and word usage are not purely scribal. They belong to normalized oral as well as written speech, and instruction in normalized speech is an odd kind of instruction to give native speakers of a language.

A native speaker hardly ever makes a mistake of grammar or of

(1966–67): 63–68; T. G. Sticht, "Learning by Listening," in *Language Comprehension and the Acquisition of Knowledge*, ed. J. B. Carroll and R. D. Freedle, (Washington, D.C., 1972), p. 72.

word usage in his native dialect. Deviations from the normalized grapholect are true mistakes only when they are also deviations from the student's own dialect, and these are almost always induced by the student's attempt to use forms outside his ken. It happens to be true that the standard language is also the standard grapholect, but it is not true that readable writing is the same as normalized, grapholectic writing. The teacher of composition is only accidentally a teacher of correctness in grammar and usage.

Should the time ever come when every child knows the grapholect as a native dialect, the composition teacher will still have a hard task. The teaching of literacy will still include instruction in genre conventions and devices of readability, and that is by itself a demanding job for teachers and students alike. When this job is compounded by the additional need to teach the conventions of a new dialect, it is an immensely difficult undertaking. It is also a necessary one. Those who scold the teacher of literacy for speeding the day when the grapholect is a native dialect for all, are defending genuine values. But they are also attacking the values of literacy and adding worry and guilt to the double burden that the teacher of literacy already carries.

Here I shall arbitrarily close my discussion of pedagogical methods. These will vary a good deal with different age groups. Since I wish to keep this book aimed at the general problems of composition, and not just at Freshman English, I will avoid further speculation about the special domain of college teaching —the only one in which I have direct experience. I have focused on three teaching methods because I think they have general applicability for all age groups. The first two methods—goal-directed commentary and revision practice—can be put in practice immediately, but the third, based on third-party evaluations, must await development of sound evaluative procedures.

Although I have stressed the need for flexibility in using these methods with different groups, I think Crews may have overstated the same point when he flatly said "that there isn't any one 'right' way to organize" a composition course.[12] That is something we don't yet know. There may in fact be a best way to organize a composition course or, at the least, a small number of ways that are better than any others. The trial-and-error approach, which I formerly advocated on the ground that we teach best when we

12. F. Crews, *Instruction Manual for The Random House Handbook* (New York, 1974), p. 1.

adapt to our students as well as to ourselves, has not brought us very far.

Improving Composition Textbooks

Since we do not yet know the best way to organize a composition course for a particular age group, we cannot possibly know the best format for a composition textbook. At present, we don't even know whether using a textbook is better than not using one. Yet if we waited for good research to give us the answers, we would wait a long time, and meanwhile we would still need to teach and learn composition. I will therefore hazard some speculations about the most useful design of textbooks, basing these on the conclusions so far recorded in this book, as well as on my practical experience in teaching and directing college composition courses. What I have to say will therefore concern mainly college texts. Whether my remarks also apply to texts for earlier grades will have to be judged by those with experience in teaching them.

We already know that textbooks are not *essential* for competent instruction in freshman composition. This inference is based on course evaluations that have been in use for several years in the composition course that I direct. These course evaluations are indirect and therefore imperfect measures of the teaching results obtained, but they do show consistent patterns for the performances of the same instructor in different sections, and they show different patterns for different instructors. Hence the evaluations appear to have a rough reliability. They show no significant correlation between good composition teaching and the use or nonuse of textbooks. But although a good instructor can do a competent job without using a textbook, the results fail to tell us whether he would have done a still better job if he had used a first-class textbook.

That textbooks are not needed is hardly surprising. An experienced teacher of any practical craft can dispense with manuals of instruction. Some teachers prefer to dispense with them, because the student's actual learning takes place in the process of producing-and-correcting, which is an individual process for each student, rather than a uniform subject matter to be gleaned from a book. On the other hand, it seems probable to me that a good manual of instruction will speed up the teaching and learning of a practical craft. My reasoning goes like this: The teacher corrects what the student produces, in order to improve the next production. The student will be best able to apply the correction (that is, alter his productive schemata) if he understands the principles behind the correction. Consulting a good manual can reinforce the teacher's explanation of the corrective principle. In this way, the manual can play the teacher's role in his absence and thereby speed up the student's progress. Hence, in ideal circumstances, where teacher and textbook share the same sound principles, a good manual should speed up the learning process.

These ideal circumstances do not yet exist, as far as I can judge. Since my principal object in this section is to speculate on how textbooks might be improved, I shall not spend much time in detailed criticism of the existing manuals. But I cannot talk about improvements without making some general remarks about the existing faults. And, since we must meanwhile use the texts that are available, I will also suggest why certain types of existing manuals are probably more useful than others.

No doubt the gravest flaw in existing texts is their lack of genuine authority. They are not based upon authoritative knowledge of the subject of composition. This is not necessarily anyone's fault. Some of the relevant knowledge about composition is scattered in a number of fields, and the rest does not yet exist. Improvements in this aspect of the manuals will come with the advancement of learning in the field.

Other flaws are more immediately correctable. It is, I would say, an absolute fault in a composition textbook to be a thick book. Those weighty volumes intimidate a student, making him assume that composition is both hard as a craft and also arduous to learn as a subject matter. In fact, the thick manuals are all padded. They preach brevity without practicing it, and they contain great amounts of irrelevant exercises and examples. Similarly, the thick source-books on grammar and usage are filled with terms unknown to many excellent writers, and are hence demonstrably unnecessary to the craft of writing. No native speaker needs to be taught lengthy refinements of grammar. The solecisms that most college students commit can be listed on a few pages. But even if these manuals and handbooks held only gold, it would be a serious pedagogical error to make them thick and therefore intimidating to their student audience. A thick composition book is pedagogically counterproductive. To use one in a composition course is analogous to lecturing on composition, and is just as inefficient.

Why do some teachers like to use these elephantine productions? When I ask my colleagues this question, I receive most often a nonpedagogical answer. The choice of a big book usually arises from the teacher's laudable decision to focus his course on composition rather than literature. The thickness of the manual then becomes the outward and visible sign of intellectual respectability in a course that eschews standard intellectual content. Very rarely does the teacher actually use a big proportion of the material in the manual. When I have commented that the pedagogical disadvantages of a thick book seem to outweigh the hoped-for advantages, my colleagues at several institutions have usually conceded my point and have resolved to examine less intimidating texts.

On the other side, it is probably a sound psychological principle to give composition intellectual respectability through the use of a good if slender manual. It serves to give the course an apparent center and an apparent authority which it might otherwise lack. It also gives common guidance to both teacher and students, through commonly shared principles and terminology. These are all significant pedagogical advantages. The danger in using even a good manual is in the subtle implication that the learning to be gained is book-learning rather than habitual schemata for practicing a craft.

Another flaw in some of the manuals, thick and thin, is their narrow focus on the college essay. Some degree of emphasis on this genre is useful because it helps motivate students. They appreciate the direct utility to themselves of learning to write papers that will earn them good grades. But this narrowness of focus tempts handbook writers into rules and maxims that are too rigid even for college essays. One of the more popular manuals, for instance, admonishes the student to state his thesis at the end of the first paragraph, to make each paragraph four or five sentences long, and to make the conclusion an "inverted funnel." No doubt a student who follows this formula will write better papers than one who has no schemata at all. But the formula will not teach him to write well. The rules have too many plausible exceptions to receive the prominence they get. A student is better served, even in learning to write college essays, by being taught maxims that are more general and fundamental. This is so because the conventions of prose genres are tolerant and variable, whereas the principles of good prose consistently govern all genres, including the college essay.

The objections I have raised against some of the existing manuals do not apply to the collections of stories and essays which supplement the manuals and serve as a source of paper topics. These "readers," as they are called, can be useful points of departure, and my only complaint against them is against their misuse. Big reading assignments are a waste of the student's time in a course whose avowed aim is instruction in the craft of writing. To hold long class discussions about the content of these readers is in my view a dereliction of duty by the teacher. (But it is true that no one can write better than he can read, since he must read his own text.) The time spent in a long discussion on some topical issue would be better spent in discussing how to revise a student's paper, or by using class time for writing. It is true that wide reading has been a good way to learn about writing. But it has always been a slow and inefficient way to learn the craft, since we quickly forget the linguistic forms of the prose we read. The best use of a reader is for occasional brief assignments that will serve as the subjects of student essays. Sometimes they can also provide examples of good writing for class analysis. But little time should be spent on readers. They, too, ought to be thin books.

What, then, is the most useful form for a college writing text? Some inferences can be drawn from what we already know. It should be a book that encourages the production-correction process between student and teacher. The maxims of correction (or revision) should be those used by the teacher and should reinforce his comments. The maxims should be sound ones, having a wide application. They should be explained persuasively, and in a form the student can apply directly to his own prose. They should be limited in number, and grouped according to their relative importance for their typical audience. The book should encourage the student to believe that he can master the elements of the craft and make future progress on his own. The book should be slender, to point up the limited number of maxims to be learned and the greater importance of actual writing and revising as compared with reading a book about writing. No existing text meets all these criteria, but one that meets several of them is *Elements of Style* by Strunk and White. Other, similar short manuals will probably work just as well.

Finally, I should stress that these inferences about desirable textbook qualities are merely informed guesses. Guesses are what we are stuck with in the absence of decisive experimental results.

Advancing Composition Research

My optimistic prediction that good research will lead to big improvements in composition will meet with warranted skepticism. Research has continued to pile up as the quality of writing has continued to decline. Composition research cannot change the television habits of the young, or encourage them to read more, or make them believe that good writing is important to learn. Research cannot transform all present teachers of writing into good writers. The best answer to these truths is that TV culture makes intensive research into composition all the more important. After all, one object of such research is to make composition teaching and learning more efficient, and thereby to make better use of the limited time that is now available for reading and writing. Inefficient methods, like spending one's days and nights in the study of Addison, could work when Addison did not compete with Archie Bunker. Efficient methods are now essential; in earlier times they were merely highly desirable.

The objection that composition research has failed in the past is a troubling one. Since there is wide agreement that the quality of this research has been low, on what grounds can we expect the quality to improve? The most hopeful augury is the present public outcry over the decline in writing skills. Public concern means increased support for an effort to reverse the decline. It also means that those who join the effort will get greater recognition than they have enjoyed in the past. This rise in the status of the subject will then help to raise the quality of composition research, because professional talent has always pursued professional status. And in the past, the professional status of composition at the universities has been at the bottom of the heap.

The danger in the new situation is that composition research will become as chaotic as the California gold rush. Good work will be as hard to find as nuggets in a well-panned stream. Duplication of effort will abound. In the long run, the gold may get sifted out, but only in the long run. Research into efficient methods in composition will be of greatest usefulness if the research effort is itself efficiently conducted. I don't suggest imposing some sort of five-year plan on creative researchers. But in order to avoid wasteful duplication of effort, I do suggest that we create machinery for keeping researchers informed about the work-in-progress of others.

We also need to introduce into the subject higher scientific standards for published work. Researchers in many fields recognize an important distinction between published work that has been subjected to careful outside scrutiny and work that has been less meticulously criticized before publication. In the past, we have had no reliable system of quality control, no refereed journals of recognized authority. And one reason for these deficiencies, besides the low status imposed upon the field, is the hybrid character of composition research. A discipline needs to exist in its own right before it achieves a tradition of high scientific standards. But composition research is not a well-defined field of study and perhaps never can become one. This creates a special but not a unique problem.

The difference between a field like composition research and a field like experimental psychology is the difference between a mission and a subject matter. The implications of this distinction have been very ably drawn by Weinberg in his book *Reflections on Big Science.* [13] The important problems in a society, Weinberg observes, are usually made up of subproblems from a number of different scientific fields. These subproblems, essential to the mission, are neglected in the fields themselves, because they are not very interesting problems within those fields. To solve one of them would not bring a scientist recognition among his peers, would not gain him tenure at a first-class university, would not advance the field itself in a significant way. In short, the subproblem does not attract an effort within the universities proportional to its social value.

An example from composition research comes easily to mind. A teacher of composition could better fulfill his mission if he knew the answer to the following question. What pattern of writing assignments will tend to promote the fastest improvements in the writing ability of college freshmen? This is a question that every composition teacher asks himself and his colleagues—a crucial question which has received no dependable answer. Is it best to assign two short papers every week? One short paper a week? To vary the length and frequency of the assignments? To stress intellectual topics? To stress personal topics? Should sentences come before paragraphs? Should there be a revision assignment after every paper? Or after every second, or third, or fourth paper? Will the best assignment pattern vary with different

13. A. Weinberg, *Reflections on Big Science* (Cambridge, Mass., 1967).

groups? If so, what is the extent of the variation? Are there typical patterns of variation? Are there methods of predicting, after a few class meetings, which assignment pattern will be best for a given class? No teacher of the subject will doubt that having reliable answers to these questions will make his teaching more effective.

But if we look at these questions from the side of the experimenter, rather than the teacher, we get a very different estimate of their interest and value. Reliable answers would be forthcoming only if the necessary experiments were conducted under the guidance of a first-class experimental psychologist, one familiar with the design of experiments and with such lurking dangers as premature conclusions, uncontrolled variables, and insufficient data bases. The psychologist would know that even early, tentative results would probably require several years of painstaking work. And he would know that, when the final results were in, they would do nothing to enhance his reputation as an experimental psychologist. They would probably have few basic implications in psychology. Their potential application would be rather limited. Hence, to a first-class experimental psychologist, the whole problem will seem trivial and uninteresting, not to say tedious, time-consuming, and messy.

Moreover, great practical difficulties would beset the undertaking. The psychologist will foresee that some dimensions of the problem are beyond his competence. Some of the crucial variables might turn out to be social in character rather than psychological, and since the best pattern of assignments might be different for different social groups, the experimenter would need the help of an expert in sociology. He would also need the assistance of an expert in educational psychology, and the cooperation of teachers, department chairmen, deans, and other college administrators. Small wonder that we still lack an answer to this crucial, innocent-looking question about effective assignment patterns in composition courses.

Weinberg suggests that this kind of deficiency in practical research can be made good by instituting mission-oriented research enterprises. Such team projects already exist outside the universities, in special laboratories, private research organizations, and industry. These extramural team efforts cut across the standard disciplines and yield rewards that are different from the standard rewards within the disciplines and the universities. Unfortunately, the pattern of extramural, team research may not work in the case of composition, since the laboratories *are* the schools and universities. Somehow, mission-oriented research in composition will need to be integrated into the universities themselves. And the universities will need to develop appropriate arrangements and incentives for conducting it.

Before the universities can institute such projects, they will need authoritative scientific guidance. It is no reflection on the national teaching organizations that they cannot easily supply this scientific expertise. The NCTE, the CCCC, and the MLA are organizations of teachers, not scientific researchers. They are not equipped to pass judgment on the quality of scientific research. They have no special competence in the organization and evaluation of large, multidiscipline scientific missions. For assistance, the universities will need to turn to institutions like the National Science Foundation, and to authoritative persons with experience in the organization of mission-oriented research. The role of the teaching organizations is to help identify the missions themselves—the goals to be achieved.

One goal at the top of everyone's list will be to develop reliable methods of evaluating the quality of writing. This is the sine qua non of all future composition research, since without it we have no way of testing anything else. We cannot find out for instance which assignment patterns yield the best results unless we can identify what the best results are. We can't find out which maxims encourage greatest progress unless we can identify progress. I shall devote my final chapter to this problem. In this section, I have tried to suggest that this and other research problems will require the cooperation of specialists from several fields. The problems are not amenable to solution by individual humanistic research, although we humanists have been called upon to solve them. We need the help of our colleagues in education, psychology, and the social sciences. We also need help from experienced organizers of mission-oriented research.

The most promising sign that this large-scale effort will be undertaken is the renewed interest in the subject of composition. For the first time in its history, the Modern Language Association now has a division devoted to composition. Professors of comparative literature are writing on the subject. Ph.D's with credentials in composition are getting teaching jobs, while Ph.D's in literary history are driving taxis. The professional status of composition teaching is rising. If this revival of interest in the subject is coupled with practical knowledge based on sound research, the general quality of writing is likely to improve. If that happens, the composition teacher will have done his share in promoting the general welfare.

7

**The Valid Assessment of
Writing Ability**

The Valid Assessment of Writing Ability

The judging of writing ability is a problem because of the great disagreement among English teachers as to the nature of good writing.

The Journal of Educational Research
64 (1970)

*Tis with our judgments as our watches: none
Go just alike, yet each believes his own.*

A. *Pope*, Essay on Criticism

It was very far from my original plan to conclude this book with a chapter on a technical research problem, for I did not foresee that writing assessment would be the single most important snag to practical progress in composition teaching and research. But even that fact would scarcely induce me to close this book with a discussion of assessment, if I had not also come to see that the assessment problem has wide dimensions which embrace some of the main arguments of the book as a whole. For instance, the argument that relative readability is the appropriate criterion of good writing must necessarily be relevant to the assessment problem; otherwise what practical use would the criterion have? Furthermore, I have come to see that the assessment problem is not merely a practical, trial-and-error affair, but that it is also a significant philosophical problem which deserves a significant place in a theoretical book. It would be gratifying if the following theoretical analysis should prove to have practical utility in solving the assessment problem sometime in the future. That remains to be seen.

The Difficulty of an Inductive Approach

Any method of writing assessment, however reliable and valid in its own terms, must also be consistent with judgments about good writing in literate society at large. Composition is taught at the behest of society—the court of last resort—and no form of professional assessment should be at odds with the verdict of that court. This is the unalterable constraint that must govern an assessment method, if it is to have any practical use in our system of education.

One of the bright spots in composition research is some very soundly conducted experimentation which has shown us how literate society does in fact judge the quality of writing. This research, published by Remondino in 1959, and by Diederich and his associates in 1961, showed that holistic judgments of writing by literate society are so highly variable that a pessimist could find grounds for despair and a cynic grounds for support of any scheme of evaluation that he preferred.[1] Here is part of Diederich's description of the experiment which he and his co-workers conducted:

> We secured 300 papers written by students in their first month at three different colleges and had them all graded by sixty distinguished readers in six occupational fields. As our academic judges we had ten college English teachers, ten social science teachers, and ten natural science teachers. As our non-academic judges we had ten writers and editors, ten lawyers, and ten business executives. . . . These were all outstanding people who were deeply concerned about the way students write. . . . Our only directions were to sort the papers into nine piles in order of general merit, using their own idea of what constituted general merit. The only rules were that all nine piles must be used, with not less than twelve papers in

1. C. Remondino, "A Factorial Analysis of the Evaluation of Scholastic Compositions in the Mother Tongue," *British Journal of Educational Psychology* 30: (1959) 242–51; P. Diederich, J. W. French, S. Carlton, "Factors in Judgments of Writing Ability," *Educational Testing Service Research Bulletin* (Princeton, N.J., 1961). See also F. I. Godshalk et al., *The Measurement of Writing Ability* (N.Y., 1966), p. 40.

any pile. Then on as many papers as possible we asked them to write brief comments on anything they liked or disliked.[2]

When the papers came back, the following results were tabulated: "out of the 300 essays graded, 101 received every grade from 1 to 9; 94 percent received either seven, eight, or nine different grades; and no essay received less than five different grades from fifty-three readers." The highest correlation within the professional groups was about .40, and English teachers were among those who showed this high (low) degree of correlation.

This last finding will confirm what most students believe, namely that their papers will often get different grades from different composition teachers. It will also explain why English teachers who are brought together to evaluate writing samples must first go through a training (or socializing) process leading to group conformity before they begin to reach agreement about the relative merits of writing samples. The Educational Testing Service creates such conformed teams in order to grade writing tests, but in light of Diederich's research it is no surprise that the "table leaders" of ETS teams must periodically confer with one another to ensure that the conformed teams are also made to conform with each other. Left to themselves, the teams cannot be depended on to bring in highly correlated results.

In his experiment, Diederich undertook to analyze the reasons behind this diversity of judgment about writing quality. He and his co-workers wanted to determine whether an analysis of results from the 300 papers could disclose an informative pattern. After a good deal of sophisticated work, they gradually reduced the number of factors to be considered; yet even in the simplified analysis the experimenters tabulated 11,018 comments on 3,357 papers under 55 headings. They ultimately identified five clusters of readers who tended to agree with each other and who disagreed with readers in every other cluster. They also discovered from the associated comments that these clusters were apparently formed according to a predominant weight given to a single main criterion. The predominant criteria identified were:

quality of ideas	16 readers
usage, sentence structure, punctuation, and spelling	13 readers

2. P. Diederich, *Measuring Growth in English*, NCTE (Urbana, Il., 1974), p. 5.

organization and analysis	9 readers
wording and phrasing	9 readers
flavor and personality	7 readers

Diederich quite properly stressed the significance of these results: "We *know* that these five qualities influenced the judgments of this particular set of readers, and I use the word *know* deliberately. These results are far more convincing than any theoretical, armchair analysis of how students ought to write."[3] Indeed they are! For the results indicate how literate society, the court of last resort, actually judges writing. Moreover, these same factors were established independently in another experiment for scores on papers that were written in Italian and judged by Italian readers.[4] That experiment yielded the same predominant traits and the same variability.

These inductively achieved results seem at first to suggest that the solution to the assessment problem will be in an analytical approach to writing assessment, one which uses the analytical categories arrived at by Remondino, and by Diederich, French, and Carlton. Before I discuss this possibility, however, I must interpose a comment on the features which any proposed solution to the assessment problem must exhibit, if the solution is to be truly useful for teaching and research.

By general agreement among experts in assessment, the two important features of any assessment method are reliability and validity. A scoring method is reliable if its results are consistent, that is, if users of the method will reach results that are "highly correlated." And the method is valid if it does indeed test the quality which the method claims to test—in this case writing quality or writing ability. For instance, the method of using "T-units" is highly reliable, because it is an objectively countable assessment method.[5] Independent counters of the average length of T-units will show high correlation with each other. But the method is inadequate because writing quality, by universal consent, has a necessary connection with the communication of meaning, while the length of a T-unit has no necessary con-

3. *Measuring Growth in English*, p. 9.
4. C. Remondino, "A Factorial Analysis."
5. A "T-Unit" is a "terminal unit," or, as normally punctuated, a sentence.

nection with the effective communication of one's meaning.[6]

What features of a writing assessment method would make it both highly reliable and highly valid? In practice, no valid method of writing assessment yet proposed has been truly reliable. The ETS method, for instance, is reliable only within a conformed group of ETS readers. A different conformed group in a different time or place could not be relied on to yield similar results. That is because, in this instance, reliability and validity are codependent. We cannot get reliable, independent agreement in the scoring of writing samples unless we also get widespread agreement about the qualities of good writing. Apparently, that is the sine qua non of a solution to the assessment problem. But as Diederich and his co-workers discovered, holistic agreement does not exist either among English teachers or in society at large. Hence reliability and validity must be sought in an analytical approach.

Although it was obvious from Diederich's inductive results that a purely holistic method of scoring could not yield the necessary reliability, it was equally obvious that any method which departed from the criteria actually used in society would be inappropriate. Diederich therefore decided on an analytical approach that would use the categories which, according to his research, actually govern the judgments of literate society. But he saw that, in order to achieve reliability, a uniform system of weighting would have to be imposed on the categories. One such system, that proposed by Diederich,[7] is shown on p. 181.

This kind of analytical system has not, however, enjoyed wide acceptance, and the reasons why such methods should have failed to make headway will help to show the difficulties of an inductive approach to the assessment problem. The great value of the inductive work of Diederich and Remondino lies in the information it has yielded, not in the determination of a method. Their work has proved two significant facts: (1) that we disagree widely in our holistic judgments of writing, and (2) that the basis of our

6. The average length of T-units does tend to indicate syntactical maturity in writing, although it does not measure the quality of writing with respect to its communicative purposes. Some first-rate expository writers (an example would be A. J. P. Taylor) habitually use short T-units. But see Kellogg Hunt, et al., *An Instrument to Measure Syntactic Maturity* (Tallahassee, Fla., 1968), and also other works by Hunt.

7. Diederich presents his system in A. Jewett and C. Bush, eds., *Improving English Composition* (National Education Association, Washington, D.C., 1965), p. 96.

disagreements seems to lie in the different weights which we attach to a few traits of writing. This means that an inductive approach cannot by itself lead to agreement, and that to impose an analytical weighting system based on the inductive results will actually work against widespread agreement. For, to use the categories about which readers *disagree* is to codify disagreement and to lose widespread acceptance from the start. An equally serious flaw in using these inductively derived analytical categories is that they pertain chiefly to just one kind of expository writing and would be inappropriate to stories or other forms of prose now taught and graded in the schools.[8]

A Scale for Grading English
Composition
___

1—Poor   2—Weak   3—Average   4—Good   5—Excellent
___

Quality and development of ideas	1 2 3 4 5		
Organization, relevance, movement	1 2 3 4 5	_____ x 5 = _____	
Style, flavor, individuality	1 2 3 4 5	Subtotal	
Wording and phrasing	1 2 3 4 5	_____ x 3 = _____	
Grammar and sentence structure	1 2 3 4 5	Subtotal	
Punctuation	1 2 3 4 5		
Spelling	1 2 3 4 5		
Form and legibility	1 2 3 4 5	_____ x 1 = _____	
		Subtotal	
		_____ %	

**A Brief Sketch of the Assessment
Problem since Plato**

Diederich's inductive procedure showed the nature but not the ultimate grounds of reader disagreements. A more complex experiment would be needed to explain those grounds. Yet, in a

8. See Charles Cooper, "Measuring Growth in Writing," *English Journal* 64: (1975) 111–20.

sense, this experiment has already been conducted on a wide scale throughout the history of literary evaluation. In that domain critics have disagreed for centuries in their holistic judgments of texts, and, since the time of Plato and Aristotle, the fundamental grounds for their disagreements have been known. The structure of the problem has remained the same, in all of its many guises, throughout the centuries.

This structure can be seen in its pure form in the contrast between the mode of evaluation practiced by Plato and the mode advanced by Aristotle. When Plato banished Homer's poetry from his ideal state, he did so on the assumption that Homer should get very high marks for organization, style, wording, and phrasing, but very low marks for the quality of his ideas. The ideas of Homer were wrong, misleading, and harmful. The effect of his writing was mainly a bad effect, and so it must be judged adversely. This platonic mode of judgment is correctly called "extrinsic evaluation," because it is based on criteria that are extrinsic to the writer's intentions, and even includes judgments about the quality of those intentions.

The Aristotelian mode, exemplified in the *Poetics*, is an almost equally pure version of *intrinsic* evaluation. It is a mode that begins and ends in the *telos* or implicit intention of the kind of writing that is judged. The quality of the text is judged according to its success in fulfilling its own implicit intentions, and these are not, by and large, to be measured against different intentions. That would be like "comparing apples and oranges," as popular Aristotelianism states the case.

In the context of this chapter, it is obvious that Aristotle's principles have a great attraction, because intrinsic evaluation is the only kind that could yield widespread agreement. Moreover, Aristotle holds further attractions for the teacher of a craft or skill as such, since intrinsic evaluation is, in principle, a judgment of one's technical success, of one's skill in accomplishing one's intentions. And, indeed, I shall propose intrinsic evaluation as the appropriate principle of assessment in composition research. But that is premature. In theoretical matters it is dangerous to disregard Plato or dismiss him. It is Plato who discloses the grounds of disagreement among readers of writing samples, and those disagreements cannot be ignored.

They are based on the truth that a purely intrinsic evaluation is inadequate for any significant judgment in human affairs. An A-plus success in achieving a trivial or harmful intention is a trivial or harmful success, and ought to be so judged. It *will* be so assessed by most of us. We do not make our significant judgments on purely intrinsic principles. Yet when we are given a task like judging student papers, we do try to introduce a large element of intrinsic evaluation. It is probable, therefore, that some of the variations in reader judgments and in the weight attached to different aspects of writing reflect different proportions of extrinsic and intrinsic judgments.

It is probable, for instance, that the sixteen readers in Diederich's experiment who laid greatest stress on the quality of ideas were judging more extrinsically than the nine readers who stressed wording and phrasing. Nor is it at all surprising that the first group formed a majority, for in our actual judgments we are mostly Platonists, and are right to be so. On the other hand, few of us are purely extrinsic judges of human productions. In the history of literary criticism since antiquity, all memorable or significant critics have combined both modes of judgment, and it is very probable that readers of student papers do the same.

For anyone interested in the standardization of judgment, this mixture of basic judicial principles is an embarrassment. For if one concedes man's variabilities of temperament and taste, one is led to the view that only intrinsic judgments can yield agreement, even though one knows that intrinsic judgments are not enough. I shall give just one historical example of this perennial embarrassment. It is exhibited by the best British theorist of the eighteenth century—David Hume—so it ought to suffice as an example. Hume confronted the problem in a short essay called "Of the Standard of Taste," which he began by conceding (as Plato and Aristotle did not need to do) the "great variety" of judgments in the world—even "greater in reality than in appearance."

Behind this variety in judgments, however, there exists a significant potential for agreement, if only the critic will

> preserve his mind free from all prejudice, and allow nothing
> to enter into his consideration, but the very object which is sub-
> mitted to his examination. We may observe that every work of
> art, in order to produce its due effect on the mind, must be
> surveyed in a certain point of view and cannot be fully relished
> by persons, whose situation, real or imaginary, is not con-
> formable to that which is required by the performance.

This special, intrinsic "point of view," is determined by regarding the work's intentions:

> Every work of art has also a certain end or purpose, for which
> it is calculated; and is to be deemed more or less perfect, as it
> is more or less fitted to attain this end. . . . These ends we must
> carry constantly in our view, when we peruse any perfor-
> mance; and we must be able to judge how far the means
> employed are adapted to their respective purposes.

That is a precise description of intrinsic judgment, but it
constitutes only one strand of the argument in Hume's essay. The
other strand takes account of our need to compare apples and
oranges—in other words to make the extrinsic judgments that
count. The need to do this leads even David Hume into a logical
tangle. On the one hand, Hume argues that we should adopt the
point of view demanded by the work. In that conception he
follows Aristotle and Alexander Pope:

> A perfect judge will read each work of wit
> With the same spirit that its author writ.
>
> . . . .
>
> In every work regard the writer's end
> Since none can compass more than they intend.[9]

But, on the other hand, we must also be able to judge between
intentions:

> Whoever would assert an equality of genius and elegance
> between Ogilby and Milton, or Bunyan and Addison, would
> be thought to defend no less an extravagance, than if he had
> maintained a molehill to be as high as Tenerife.

And here one no longer adopts the point of view demanded by
the work, but instead adopts a normal human point of view
which could be compared to the healthy normal state of the eye
or ear:

> If in the sound state of the organ, there be an entire or con-
> siderable uniformity of sentiment among men, we may thence
> derive an idea of the perfect beauty; in like manner as the
> appearance of objects in daylight, to the eye of a man in
> health, is denominated their true and real color.

Now the logical tangle here is the difference between "the
sound state of the organ" and the special "point of view which the
performance supposes." The one judgment is Platonic, the other
Aristotelian. Both are indeed required—but in what proportion,

---

9. Pope, *Essay on Criticism*, 11. 233–34; 255–56.

what balance? Hume does not and cannot tell us, and he therefore fails to give us an adequate standard of judgment even in principle. That is to say, he cannot give us a holistic standard that combines both extrinsic and intrinsic criteria. The point, then, of this historical example is to draw the following moral: the problem of holistic assessment has been studied by some of the greatest thinkers of history. They have not solved the problem, because it is not susceptible of solution. For that reason, and for purposes of research, we must restrict ourselves to judgments where agreement can be reached in principle, that is, to intrinsic judgment.

Before I proceed to draw some practical conclusions, I shall first discuss some objections to intrinsic judgments of writing. I want to acknowledge and answer those objections before they arise insistently in the reader's mind, so that I can go forward without pausing over them during the exposition.

In composition, the main objection to purely intrinsic judgments of writing is a pedagogical one. If a composition teacher gives a student a high mark whenever he expresses well what he aimed to express, the student will quickly learn to limit his aims. He will write trivial and simple A papers, instead of writing ambitious, difficult C papers which would tax him and develop his skill in writing and thinking. His true progress in writing could be slowed down instead of being speeded up. Moreover, it is palpably unfair for the teacher to give a high grade to a successful simple paper and a lower grade to a paper that succeeds slightly less well in accomplishing a more difficult aim.

These pedagogical objections are altogether convincing, but a teacher can deal with them quite successfully in any of three ways: (1) by using "closed" assignments, where the paper's aims are defined in advance; (2) by using an extrinsic *category* where qualities of thought and intention are scored separately and made part of the grade; (3) by using a "difficulty factor," as in the scoring of diving competitions. (The use of this method in the 1976 Olympic diving competition led to a remarkable uniformity of purely intrinsic scores for individual dives.)

The pedagogical reasons, then, for adding extrinsic judgments are compelling, but equally compelling are the pedagogical reasons for *isolating* them from intrinsic judgments. To the extent that one is teaching and nurturing skill in writing, one needs to diagnose the student's strengths and weaknesses in that skill, quite apart from his other skills. That is true regardless of the relative importance which one attaches to different educational goals. Moreover, the student's motivation to improve his writing is likely to be enhanced if he has confidence in the way his skill is being analyzed and evaluated. And since intrinsic evaluation is the only kind of assessment in which *anyone* should have confidence, it is pedagogically desirable to separate it from extrinsic evaluation. The extrinsic quality and the difficulty of a student's intentions can be influenced by the teacher in the ways that I have already mentioned. If that is done, no compelling objection can be raised against using intrinsic assessment in composition teaching. On the contrary, there are compelling pedagogical advantages in using it to secure the student's confidence in the fairness and reliability of the teacher's assessments.

The Use of Deductive Categories of Assessment

My analysis of the assessment problem has so far been primarily an analysis of its logical structure. That is an essential first step. But I also believe that a logical, deductive approach will prove helpful in taking the second step, namely, the determination of the most useful *categories* of writing assessment. We have already seen that an inductive development of assessment categories did not work. On the other hand, the advantages to be gained from *deductive*, a priori categories are their applicability to a chosen goal, and their potential for widespread acceptance, as based on their intuitive appeal.

I believe that the following deductive categories can meet these criteria.

1. The quality of intentions.
2. The quality of their presentation.
3. Correctness.

From my earlier remarks it will be obvious that (1) corresponds to what I have called extrinsic evaluation, while (2) corresponds to the intrinsic evaluation of writing. Number (3) also belongs to intrinsic evaluation, but it requires a separate category because of the special rules that attach to the written medium. These rules of spelling, punctuation, capitalization, and, perhaps of grammar, constitute a separable dimension in the teaching of composition. Errors in this dimension are precisely identifiable and even countable. The weight that should be attached to such errors will

vary according to the pedagogical circumstances, and this variability will make combined scorings of (2) and (3) unreliable.
Moreover, since the teaching of correctness is often a matter of
drill and memorization, one may reasonably score it apart from
skill of presentation, an art which one teaches very differently.
For these same reasons, a large-scale test which separates the two
categories will be more informative for composition research than
a test which scores (2) and (3) together.

I would hazard the conjecture that a further breakdown of
category (2) would *not* be useful to the teacher or the researcher.
The importance of such elements as vocabulary, sentence structure and length, flavor, and so on will vary greatly in different
pieces of writing—a telling objection to elaborate analytical
categories. Another objection to a further breakdown of category
(2) is the time consumed by elaborate scoring methods. If holistic
scoring proves to be adequate for assessing quality of presentation, then holistic scoring in this category recommends itself on
theoretical as well as practical grounds. For in theory, no other
method could cope with the varying importance of different
elements in different pieces of writing.

In sum, holistic scoring of category (2), *intrinsic quality of
presentation*, has at least a sporting chance of solving the
assessment problem—if the problem can be solved. No other
scoring principle has even this sporting chance, for intrinsic
evaluation is the only kind of assessment that can yield widespread agreement in our heterogeneous world.

These considerations have now considerably narrowed the
focus of the assessment problem. Everything will hinge on
whether wide agreement can be reached regarding the scoring
and also the centrality of category (2). The most important
consideration in its favor is that the object of assessment in
composition is writing ability, not the overall quality of writing
samples per se. In the pedagogical context, the purpose of the
sample is to yield inferences about how well the student will write
still further "samples" in a variety of writing situations beyond
the composition class. The purpose of instruction in writing is to
develop this transferable skill, whether the subject is "What I Did
Last Summer" or "Why Students Cheat."

Another corollary point is less obvious and perhaps less well-
known. A student will exhibit far greater variations in the quality
of his ideas and aims than in the quality of his presentations. One
topic is more productive of good thinking for student A than for

student B, and a different topic will reverse these results. This has been established convincingly in researches by Freedman and Nold.[10] I do not suggest that these variations in productive thinking will fail to affect the student's quality of presentation per se, but I do suggest that such variations will affect it far less than they affect holistic scores which include category (1). In other words, a score on category (2), intrinsic quality of presentation, is a better index of *writing ability* than a holistic score which includes category (1). These arguments for the centrality of intrinsic evaluation in composition teaching and research seem to me decisive.

A Promising Approach to Solving the Assessment Problem

Now the *principle* of intrinsic evaluation is already practiced very widely as an essential feature of composition teaching. One of the teacher's refrains is: "I know what you *wanted* to say, but you didn't actually *say* it," which is a paradox, since the writer did "say" it; otherwise the teacher couldn't have guessed his intentions. The paradoxical side of the situation is overlooked by both parties, because guesses about intentions are inherent in our understanding of all speech, spoken or written.

It is true that our guesses about the aims of a poor writer are often highly tentative and uncertain, which is chiefly why we judge him to be a poor writer. But in many cases we *are* confident of having correctly guessed the complex aims of the writer. Is that not in itself a sufficient warrant for a high score in category (2)? Intuitively, we know that this is *not* a sufficient criterion for intrinsic judgment. We need an intrinsic standard beyond the blunt criterion that the writer has achieved his aims. We need a standard for judging his *degree* of success in achieving his various intentions.

In the body of this book I have argued that such a standard is inherent in speech and can be inferred from the history of

10. Sara W. Freedman and Ellen Nold, "A Multivariate Analysis of Readers' Responses to Essays," *Research in the Teaching of English*, forthcoming. I thank the authors for sending me their preprint as well as their raw data. The latter showed big variations in the performances of certain students, depending on the topic assigned. Of the twenty-two students tested, nine showed this tendency, which has also been reported in F. I. Godshalk et al., *The Measurement of Writing Ability*, p. 13.

language and the history of prose. The universal standard by which we judge the relative success of an achieved aim in speech is the standard of least effort. If the very same complex of aims is achieved by the writer with less reader effort, then it is to that extent an intrinsically more successful piece of writing. I have also shown in earlier chapters that this standard of intrinsic effectiveness correlates very well with the maxims of good prose which intuition and experience have educed over the centuries. In short, the intrinsic standard for judging a writer's *degree* of success in fulfilling his aims is the standard of relative readability.

This means that our categories of writing assessment can be usefully reformulated as follows:

A. *Extrinsic evaluation*
   1. Quality of intentions
B. *Intrinsic evaluation*
   2. Relative readability or intrinsic effectiveness
   3. Correctness

This restatement of category (2), towards which the whole argument of the book has led, ought to have some significant practical implication for teaching and research. For, judgments based on this reformulation of category (2) are theoretically confirmable by objective methods that are independent of judgments by individual readers. If this theoretical possibility should prove to be a practical reality, then we might at last be able to achieve a high degree of validity and reliability in judging a person's writing ability on the basis of a sample of his writing.

Now this optimistic prophecy would be fulfilled only if relative readability could be definitely scored, and that is not yet certain. My colleagues and I are beginning to tackle this problem, which is far more complex than the problem of scoring absolute readability by means of cloze tests or readability formulas. On the other hand, our first trials are promising, and we see no insuperable barrier to the practical fulfillment of the theoretical possibilities. For what is involved in the theoretical basis of the scoring method is also involved in our practical judgments of writing. We make inferences about what a writer is trying to "say" when we judge how well he has said it.

At this early stage of our experimentation, it would be premature to give a detailed account of a method to score relative readability. I shall mention only a few of the principles which make the attempt seem feasible. At present the most important principles seem to be (1) the dependable correlation between absolute readability and absolute listenability; (2) the control of audience processing-time through taped oral presentation; (3) the possibility of expertly rewriting most papers, while keeping synonymous the complex intentions of the two versions; (4) the accurate comparison of audience uptake from the two versions (including tone, implicit attitudes, and so on) by means of a "threshold questionnaire"; (5) the independent duplicability of the comparative scores when using different audiences, different research teams, different rewrites, and different threshold questionnaires.[11] These laborious methods are, of course, unusable in the classroom, but they might have a very practical use in testing and certifying the reliability of writing assessors.

I shall therefore carry my optimistic prophecy still further. If we could definitively determine the relative readability of a writing sample, we could also determine by a test the assessment abilities of those who were asked to score test samples from a particular age group. An assessor who consistently gave correct scores to these heterogeneous samples could be relied on to agree independently with the scores of any other assessor who also gave consistently correct scores to the test samples. Such readers could then be certified as reliable assessors of writing samples. Their agreement about future samples would be independent of mere team conformity; the evaluations would be similar even though the assessors were widely separated in time and space. The reason for their agreement would be that their scores were, in a very legitimate sense, correct scores. Their agreement would be founded on a theoretically sound normative standard. Such certified assessors could then be relied on to evaluate research into different, pedagogical methods. Hence, in well-designed pedagogical experiments, evaluations of results could be duplicated by other experimenters and could be confidently applied to the teaching of writing.

Our results to date suggest that an assessor can accurately score relative readability after a few days of practice, once he has understood the nature of the assessment criterion. If a few persons can learn to give accurate scores of intrinsic effectiveness, so can many persons. The talents required for such assessments do

11. A description of our preliminary work is outlined in "A Method for Forming Tests to Certify Assessors of Writing Ability," E. D. Hirsch, Jr., 1976. A copy of this provisional description is available on request from the Department of English, Wilson Hall, University of Virginia, Charlottesville, Va. 22901.

not exceed the capacities of most teachers. Moreover, the widespread use of intrinsic assessments by teachers as part of their grading would give all of us who teach composition a core of common purposes and common principles. Both teaching and research might then make significant progress. Many of us already judge writing according to its communicative effectiveness with respect to its communicative aims, that is, according to its relative readability. This justifies a guarded optimism about the future of composition research and about its effectiveness in raising the competence of teachers and writers alike—even if such research might also show, as it probably will, that distinguished composition teaching is an art, which, like distinguished writing, defies codification.

Index

Index